"THE SPARKLING IS NICE..."

"IT IS..."

SAKURA AND LINZE LOOKED AT THE MAGIC PARTICLES BEING RELEASED FROM THE PURETREE'S LEAVES, WHICH WERE QUITE BEAUTIFUL.

n Another World With My Smartphone 19

In Another World With My Smartphone

Patora Fuyuhara
illustration · Eiji Usatsuka

Luli

The fourth of Touya's summoned Heavenly Beasts. She is the Azure Monarch, the ruler of dragons. She often clashes with Kohaku due to her condescending personality.

Kougyoku

The third of Touya's summoned Heavenly Beasts. She is the Flame Monarch, ruler of feathered things. Though her appearance is flashy and extravagant, she's actually quite cool and collected.

Sango and Kokuyou

The second of Touya's summoned Heavenly Beasts. They are the Black Monarch, two in one. The rulers of scaled beasts. They can freely manipulate water. Sango is a tortoise, and Kokuyou is a snake. Sango is a female, and Kokuyou is a male (but he's very much a female at heart).

Kohaku

The first of Touya's summoned Heavenly Beasts. She's the White Monarch, the ruler of beasts, the guardian of the West and a beautiful White Tiger. She can create devastating shockwaves, and also change size at will.

High Rosetta

Terminal Gynoid in charge of the Workshop, one of the Babylon relics. She's called Rosetta for short. Her Airframe Serial Number is #27. For whatever reason, she's the most reliable of the bunch.

Francesca

Terminal Gynoid in charge of the Hanging Garden, one of the Babylon relics. She's called Cesca for short. Her Airframe Serial Number is #23. She likes to tell very inappropriate jokes.

Mochizuki Moroha

The God of Swords. Claims to be Touya's older sister. She trains and advises the knights of Brunhild. She's gallant and brave, but also a bit of an airhead at times.

Mochizuki Karen

The God of Love. Claims to be Touya's older sister. She stays in Brunhild because she says she needs to catch a servile god, but doesn't really do all that much in the way of hunting him. She's a total pain in the butt.

Pamela Noel

Terminal Gynoid in charge of the Tower, one of the Babylon relics. She's called Noel for short and wears a jersey. Her Airframe Serial Number is #25. She sleeps all the time, and eats lying down. Her tremendous laziness means she doesn't do all that much.

Preliora

Terminal Gynoid in charge of the Rampart, one of the Babylon relics. She's called Liora for short and wears a blazer. Her Airframe Serial Number is #20. She's the oldest of the Babylon Gynoids, and would attend to the... personal night-time needs of Doctor Babylon herself. She has no experience with men.

Fredmonica

Terminal Gynoid in charge of the Hangar, one of the Babylon relics. She's called Monica for short. Her Airframe Serial Number is #28. She's a funny little hard worker who has a bit of a casual streak. She's a good friend of Rosetta, and is the Gynoid with the most knowledge of the Frame Gears.

Bell Flora

Terminal Gynoid in charge of the Alchemy Lab, one of the Babylon relics. She's called Flora for short and wears a nurse outfit. Her Airframe Serial Number is #21. A nurse with dangerously big boobs and even more dangerous medicines.

Doctor Regina Babylon

An ancient genius from a lost civilization, reborn into an artificial body that resembles a small girl. She is the "Babylon" that created the many artifacts and forgotten technologies scattered around the world today. Her Airframe serial number is #29. she remained in stasis for five-thousand years before finally being awakened.

Atlantica

Terminal Gynoid in charge of the Research Lab, one of the Babylon relics. She's called Tica for short and wears a blazer. Her Airframe serial number is #22. Of the Babylon Numbers, she is the one who best embodies Doctor Babylon's inappropriately perverse side.

Lileleparshe

Terminal Gynoid in charge of the Storehouse, one of the Babylon relics. She's called Parshe for short and wears a shrine maiden outfit. Her Airframe Serial Number is #26. She's tremendously clumsy, even if she's just trying to help. The amount of stuff she ruins is troublingly high.

Irisfam

Terminal Gynoid in charge of the Library, one of the Babylon relics. She's called Fam for short and wears a school uniform. Her Airframe Serial Number is #24. She's a total book fanatic and hates being interrupted when she's reading.

Character Profiles

Elze Silhoueska

One of Touya's fiancees.
The elder of the twin sisters saved by Touya some time ago. A ferocious melee fighter, she makes use of gauntlets in combat. Her personality is fairly to-the-point and blunt. She can make use of Null fortification magic, specifically the spell [Boost]. She loves spicy foods.

Yumina Urnea Belfast

One of Touya's fiancees.
Princess of the Belfast Kingdom. She was twelve years old in her initial appearance, and her eyes are heterochromatic. The right is blue, while the left is green. She has mystic eyes that can discern the true character of an individual. She has three magical aptitudes: Earth, Wind, and Darkness. She's also extremely proficient with a bow and arrow. She fell in love with Touya at first sight.

Mochizuki Touya

A highschooler who was accidentally murdered by God. He's a no-hassle kind of guy who likes to go with the flow. He's not very good at reading the atmosphere, and typically makes rash decisions that bite him in the ass. His mana pool is limitless, he can flawlessly make use of every magical element, and he can cast any Null spell that he wants. He's currently the Grand Duke of Brunhild.

Sushie Urnea Ortlinde

One of Touya's fiancees.
She was ten years old in her initial appearance. Her nickname is Sue. The niece of Belfast's king, and Yumina's cousin. Touya saved her from being attacked on the road. She has an innocently adventurous spirit.

Lucia Leah Regulus

One of Touya's fiancees.
The Third Princess of the Regulus Empire, she's Yumina's age. She fell in love with Touya when he saved her during a coup. She likes to fight with twin blades, and she's on good terms with Yumina.

Kokonoe Yae

One of Touya's fiancees.
A samurai girl from the far eastern land of Eashen, a country much like Japan. She tends to repeat herself and speak formally, she does. Yae is quite a glutton, eating more than most normal people would dare touch. She's a hard worker, but can sometimes slack off. Her family runs a dojo back in Eashen, and they take great pride in their craft. It's not obvious at first, but her boobs are pretty big.

Linze Silhoueska

One of Touya's fiancees.
The younger of the twin sisters saved by Touya some time ago. She wields magic, specifically from the schools of Light, Water, and Fire. She finds talking to people difficult due to her own shy nature, but she is known to be surprisingly bold at times. Rumors say she might be the kind of girl who enjoys male on male romance... She loves sweet foods.

Paula

A stuffed toy bear animated by years upon years of the [Program] spell. She's the result of two-hundred years of programmed commands, making her seem like a fully aware living being. Paula... Paula's the worst!

Sakura

A mysterious girl Touya rescued in Eashen. She had lost her memories, but has now finally gotten them back. Her true identity is Farnese Forneus, daughter of the Xenoahs Overlord. Currently living a peaceful life in Brunhild, and she has joined the ranks of Touya's fiancees.

Leen

One of Touya's fiancees.
Former Clan Matriarch of the Fairies, she now serves as Brunhild's Court Magician. She claims to be six-hundred-and-twelve years old, but looks tremendously young. She can wield every magical element except Darkness, meaning her magical proficiency is that of a genius. Leen is a bit of a light-hearted bully.

Hildegard Minas Lestia

One of Touya's fiancees.
First Princess of the Knight Kingdom Lestia. Her swordplay talents earned her a reputation as a 'Knight Princess'. Touya saved her life when she was attacked by a group of Phrase, and she's loved him ever since. She's a good friend of Yae, and she stammers a bit when flustered.

IN ANOTHER WORLD WITH MY SMARTPHONE: VOLUME 19
by Patora Fuyuhara

Translated by Andrew Hodgson
Edited by DxS

Copyright © 2019 Patora Fuyuhara
Illustrations by Eiji Usatsuka

Original Japanese edition published in 2019 by Hobby Japan
This English edition is published by arrangement with Hobby Japan, Tokyo

English translation © 2019 J-Novel Club LLC

Find more books like this one at www.j-novel.club!

Managing Director: Samuel Pinansky
Light Novel Line Manager: Chi Tran
Managing Editor: Jan Mitsuko Cash
Managing Translator: Kristi Fernandez
QA Manager: Hannah N. Carter
Marketing Manager: Stephanie Hii

ISBN: 978-1-7183-5018-2
Printed in Korea
First Printing: December 2021
10 9 8 7 6 5 4 3 2 1

Contents

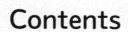

The Story So Far!

Mochizuki Touya, wielding a smartphone customized by God himself, continues to live his life in a new world. After many adventures, Touya, now Grand Duke of a small nation named Brunhild, has joined forces with the other world leaders. Why? To stop the incoming extradimensional threat known as the Phrase. These merciless invaders from another world will stop at nothing until they get what they desire. As Touya continued to investigate potential ways to repel this threat, he found himself falling into another world entirely. This Reverse World was like a mirrored version of the world he knew, and relied on a mysterious mechanical technology known as the Gollems. Now, the fate of two worlds may hang in the balance...

N

Rhea Kingdom
Greencity, Fern ◉

Rephan Kingdom

Primula Kingdom
Capital City, ◉
Primlet

Zadonia,
Land of Ice

Panaches
Kingdom
◉ Capital,
Panacelia

Triharan Holy
Empire

Gem Kingdom

Dauburn,
Land of Fire

◉ Holy Capital,
Trinity

Nation of
Orphen

◉ Martial City, Lasseif

The Allent
Theocracy

Curiela
Kingdom

Lassei Military
Kingdom

Strain Kingdom

◉ Holy Capital,
Allen

Capital City, ◉
Sitonia

Langeais
Kingdom

Gandhilis,
The Steel
Nation

◉ Imperial Capital,
Garresta

Gardio
Empire

Magitech Capital, ◉
Isenberg

He
Land'

The Worlds of
In Another World With My Smartphone
World Map

Palerius Island

I City, ous

Kingdom of Palouf

Capital City, Xenoskull
The Demon Kingdom, Xenoahs

Capital City, Slanien

The Kingdom of Elfrau

e Kingdom of Lihnea — Capital City, Nimue

Capital City, Hanookhs

The Kingdom of Hannock

The Nokia Kingdom

Yulong Remnants

Bern, The Imperial City

The Regulus Empire

Gallaria, Heart of the Empire

Divine Nation of Eashen

se

The Kingdom of Belfast

Alephis, The Royal Capital

← The Duchy of Brunhild

The Roadmare Union

Capital City, Falma

The Kingdom of Horn

Reflet

The Kingdom of Mismede

The Ramissh Theocracy

The Holy City, Isla

Capital City, Paneramare

The Kingdom of Felsen

Berge, Capital of Beasts

The Sea of Trees

Capital City, Atryle →

The Kingdom of Ryle

Capital City, Lestein →

The Knight Kingdom of Lestia

Dragoness Island

The Kingdom of Sandora

Retrobamba

Kyuray, The Sandy Capital

The Kingdom of Egret

New World

The territory formerly known as the Reverse World covered the western half of the new world. And there were two troublesome nations within that area.

Dauburn, Land of Fire, and Zadonia, Land of Ice.

These two nations had a blood feud that stretched back several generations. Each side considered the other to be thieves.

According to the world leaders I'd spoken to, the regular citizens of these nations didn't really have a problem with each other. The feud was perpetuated by the nobles, for the most part.

Each country blamed the other for the theft of an offering they'd made to their respective gods. Apparently, the theft had triggered curses that turned Dauburn into a burning hellscape and Zadonia into a frozen wasteland.

My personal theory was that gods hadn't been responsible for the problems at all. It was much more likely the work of spirits, which meant something had most likely irritated them a few hundred years ago.

"That's why I'm here to ask about what happened."

"Oh... That's, well…"

"That's hard to answer…"

I'd used my divine abilities to warp myself to the spirit realm. I floated amidst a milky-white, sparkling backdrop with the spirits of ice and flame in front of me. They were sitting on the other side of the table I'd prepared. I'd also brought a plate of cookies as a gift.

The Flame Spirit was second in the elemental hierarchy to the Fire Spirit. Much like the pillar spirit, she was a tomboyish and energetic girl with short red hair. She looked so similar to the Fire Spirit that I'd have believed them to be sisters.

The Ice Spirit was also right below her respective pillar spirit in terms of hierarchy. She was apparently akin to a sister to Shirahime of Eashen's mother, the Snow Spirit. Her hair was an icy blue, and it was styled into a princess cut. Her expression was also somewhat devoid of emotion, but given her status as a spirit, that probably shouldn't have been so surprising.

"I remember we were incarnated around five hundred years ago. But neither of us remember too much from back then. Perhaps I was irritated at some point, but I honestly can't recall."

"Indeed, I feel much the same. Given that our spiritual dependents have settled and made the environments so volatile, something must have happened there… But I can't really say for sure what that something was."

Damn, so they don't even know what the score is… Spirits were timeless beings. They reincarnated every thousand years or so, but each cycle erased their memory and appearance. They could even change from male to female or vice versa. So even if they were the ones who had cursed the two nations, assuming it was a curse, there wasn't anything they could tell me.

"It's true we don't remember much, but we could call our servile spirits back and stabilize their environments if you'd like."

"Hm… That could work, but hold off on it for now. I don't think that'd solve any of the real issues going on over there."

They weren't exactly fighting with each other over the weather, after all. Plus, suddenly changing the area without any warning was more likely to cause harm than good.

Honestly, I had a feeling that it wasn't a curse plaguing the countries... Slowly adjusting their environments back to something a bit more neutral could very well have fixed everything, but I definitely wasn't counting on it.

"You two aren't enemies or anything, are you?"

"I wouldn't say so. We hang out with each other and get along, don't we?"

"Yeah, we do. However... I can't exactly say for sure that we were friends in our previous incarnations. We change as people after each rebirth."

That made sense. They were essentially different people each time they were reborn, so it was entirely possible they were enemies in a past life.

"We heard from the spirits that knew our past selves that we were amicable back then, though. We weren't as close as we are right now, but we also weren't enemies."

"Indeed, I heard something similar from Her Watership."

Hrmph... Well, this doesn't really answer any of my questions. Guess I can't solve anything here.

Still, it's not on me to fix Dauburn and Zadonia's problems, right? I've got no reason to stick my nose into their business. If I can work out the reason, then I can fix it... But I don't really have to try too hard to figure it out.

"Sorry for taking up your time. Please take these cookies as thanks. You guys should share them with the other spirits later on."

I passed some more cookies to the two spirits before leaving the spirit realm. In the end, I learned nothing new about the cause of the old feud. It would probably have been easier to just kidnap the two leaders, and then dump them some place where they were all alone. If they had to rely on each other to survive on a deserted island, then they would be forced to grow closer.

"Haha... There's no way I'd do that...right? Ahaha..."

That sounded a little harsh, even by my standards. I shrugged a bit and headed off to Babylon, figuring I'd save that tactic as a last resort.

I arrived in the garden just in time to catch a tea party.

"Welcome to the garden, Master. I'll bring the tea over."

"Ah, thanks."

Cesca was standing below the gazebo in her maid garb as she suddenly warped away. She'd likely transported down to the castle to get some more cups.

I sat down at the table, on a chair between Yumina and Yae.

"Where were you this time, Touya?"

"I was in the spirit realm. I wanted to talk to the spirits of flame and ice, but I couldn't get much out of them."

"Did you mean to get involved with those irksome countries that are fighting over being too hot and too cold, did you?"

They're not fighting over their climates... But they're definitely irksome.

"What were you all discussing?"

"We've been talking about recent events. There's actually something I wanted to ask you, darling."

"Hm? What'd you need?"

Leen set her cup down and glanced my way. Everyone at the table followed her line of sight... I was curious about what they wanted to say.

"When you got engaged to us, you said you'd marry us once you turned eighteen, remember?"

"Uh... Yeah. That's right."

"Well, we all learned something from Karen recently. There's a difference between the world you came from and this one.

You knew it all along, didn't you? That the number of days in a year is different here." Leen looked at me with a soft, accusatory gaze. My blood ran cold as I stared back, sweat beading on my brow.

"Heh. If we go by the calendar of your world, you turned eighteen quite some time ago, didn't you?"

...Shit, they know. They goddamn know... Ugh! Karen, why'd you have to screw me over like this? They were right, though. I hadn't realized it initially, but a year in this world was a bit longer than a year on earth. Roughly four months longer, to be exact. A year in this world had sixteen months.

Initially, when I saw a thirteenth month show up on my smartphone, I couldn't believe my eyes. I ended up secretly asking Kousaka about it, just to verify.

I'd always used my smartphone to check the date and time, so I'd never seen the calendars used in this world. Plus, the fact that this world didn't have cyclical seasons didn't exactly help, either. Ever since I learned about the extended year, I'd been working off the timeframe of this world. And by the timeframe of this world, I was only seventeen years old!

But yeah... Back in the world I came from, I'd have already turned eighteen a while back.

"I-I wasn't hiding it or anything! I just figured, since I live here now, I should count my age based on the calendar of this world. I mean, heck, if we go by my world's calendar, Yumina, who's fourteen right now, would actually be eighteen already! And don't get me started on you, Leen. You'd be—"

"That's quite enough, darling..." Leen smiled as she spoke, but I sensed a murderous glint in her eyes. The pressure she could exert was nothing to scoff at.

"Okay..."

"S-Still, that means we can marry you now, doesn't it?" Linze chimed in, a light blush on her face.

"In the end, that's up to our darling, but it's a little difficult given current events. We have the wicked god to contend with, so that would cause complications…"

"Complications? Of what kind?" Yae raised an eyebrow in response to Leen's statement.

"W-Well… If we were to be impregnated, we'd have to avoid direct combat…"

HOLD UP, LEEN. YOU'RE DEFINITELY JUMPING THE GUN A BIT. Plus, you're a fairy, so you're not even very fertile!

Leen's reddened face began to spread across the table, infecting the cheeks of each of my fiancees. Naturally, the blushing sickness caught hold of me, as well.

I caught sight of Sue from the corner of my eye. She was sipping juice as casually as she could, but even her cheeks were stained red… I was a little amazed at how quickly she'd matured.

"W-Well, let's just set that aside for a minute. I'm sorry I didn't mention the age thing, but we can't get married until I've dealt with the wicked god. That's why I want to deal with it as soon as we possibly can."

"Do you think we can win, do you?"

"So long as we manage to counteract the divine venom, we'll be fine. Even if the enemy absorbed a god, it was still a NEET god that sat at the lowest standing in terms of divinity. Sure, I may look like an average Joe, but I'm still a beneficiary of God Almighty. Plus, I have seven gods in human form as backup. If I can't win with all that help, then I probably don't deserve to."

I liked to think I wasn't that incompetent. Plus, this whole thing was basically a test from God Almighty. The outcome would determine whether or not I became this world's new caretaker.

It suddenly occurred to me that Yula might not have been aware of the full scope of the situation. He probably didn't know that the god he'd managed to catch was just a pathetic NEET.

Given how egotistical that shitty NEET was, he never would've admitted something so humiliating, even under threat of death. Hell, I wouldn't have been surprised if he'd tried to pass himself off as the god of worlds or something. Yeah, that definitely sounds like something that idiot would've done.

"Oh, that's right. Lu recently awakened to a special ability gained from being a beneficiary!" Elze spoke up, prompting me to look over at Lu.

"Huh, she did?"

"Ah, yes. Th-Though it isn't a combat-related ability..." Lu smiled wryly.

The beneficiary trait was a unique ability that manifested within people as blessings from the gods that nurtured them. Lu and the rest of my fiancees were unique, since they had the potential to awaken as beneficiaries of eight gods. Those gods being myself, Karen, Moroha, Kousuke, Sousuke, Karina, Suika, and Takeru.

Still, they didn't draw their new powers from everyone at once. For example, taking me out of the equation, Sakura definitely had a closer affinity to Sousuke than anyone else. They went out to perform together, after all.

Yae and Hilde were closer to Moroha, and Elze was closer to the combat god.

Still, the main source of their divine blessing was me. The beneficiary trait was basically a gift from the gods. It was a power that elevated one beyond humanity. Yumina had her foresight, Sakura had enhanced hearing... I wondered what Lu had manifested.

"Um, well... It's my sense of taste. It's much more heightened than it used to be. I can tell different ingredients apart. I innately know what was involved in cooking something, as well as how much of it."

Wow... That's quite the skill... Lu cooked a lot with our head chef, Crea. Her ability as a cook was already right up there among the pros, despite the fact that she hadn't ever wielded a kitchen knife before meeting me. It seemed like beneficiary traits elevated innate strengths, even if they didn't know about them.

"Lu's really amazing. She managed to detect the presence of a single grain of salt that had mixed into a cup of water."

"That's definitely interesting... But wouldn't it be bad if you ate something that didn't taste good? Wouldn't it be amplified?"

"Oh, no... It doesn't activate if I don't want to. It's sort of like something I can switch on and off."

"Mm... It's the same for me... If I don't focus, I don't hear too much extra..." Sakura nodded at Lu. It was interesting that they could toggle their abilities, but I was glad they could. Having them on permanently would have been rough. Their toggle was kind of like how I could turn my divine sight on and off.

"That's pretty cool! Hey, Touya! Give me my ability too!"

"I-It doesn't exactly work like that..." I laughed softly at Sue's request. Beneficiary traits depended on the person, so there wasn't really one thing you could do to manifest it. I understood her feelings on the matter, but I couldn't do anything to speed up the process.

"U-Um... Could it be that we're slower to awaken because we've received less love?" Linze timidly spoke up.

"Hold it! You've got it all wrong! It just awakens differently depending on the person!" I didn't want them doubting my feelings, so I screamed that response at the top of my lungs. It really wasn't a nice thought.

"It's likely easier for sensory skills to manifest, rather than more physical traits."

"Yeah, what Hilde said. Yumina, Sakura, and Lu have all manifested traits related to their senses. Vision, hearing, and taste."

"I don't know if I'd call foresight related to the sense of vision…"

"It's still something you see, isn't it? I have a feeling that Hilde, Yae, and Elze will get a more physical blessing."

Probably something like improving their physical prowess… Oh, wait. That's kind of already happened. Even Sue, who was weak to begin with, could now move in tandem with our knights. And that was without any formal training. Yae, Elze, and Hilde were far above that in terms of physical prowess. The blessing they'd received was clear from that alone.

…You know, now that I think about it, our kids are gonna be super overpowered. They'd be demi-gods right off the bat, right? Then they'd have the blessing of a bunch of gods like Karen and the others… Raising them is probably gonna be hell.

…They're all gonna be girls too. Yeesh. Hopefully, they grow up with style and grace.

"I wonder what a more physical blessing would be like, I do."

"Maybe something like Elze's [**Boost**] spell?"

"Bwuh… But I already have that! I'd like something more unique!"

The physical trio started having a lively discussion about how their newfound powers would manifest. And frankly, I was a bit scared of whatever ferocious powers they'd unlock.

"Y-You don't think we'll sprout wings all of a sudden, do you?"

"N-No, that won't happen to you guys. Even when I go full divine mode, only my hair grows out. It's not that intense…" I quickly shot down Linze's strange suggestion.

Then again, having white wings would definitely make the girls look more angelic...which would fit their status as divine beneficiaries.

"Wings sound boring! I bet I'll get a trait that makes me a whole lot taller... A trait that gives me a big chest and makes me beautiful like Karen!"

...No, Sue. I don't think so. You're not describing a trait here, you're describing a full-body transformation.

You know, I'm a little surprised Sue's worrying about things like bust size... Then again, she's already twelve, so I guess those anxieties aren't uncommon. I looked back to Sue, who was patting her own budding chest.

"I wonder if I'll get as big as Flora someday..."

"...You probably shouldn't compare yourself to mythical boobs like hers. They're not a product of the natural world!" Elze quickly piped up in response to Sue.

Flora, the manager of the alchemy lab. They definitely had to be over a hundred... Maybe even a hundred and twenty. Despite their massive size, those honkers gracefully bent the laws of gravity. Those terrifying titties were well-rounded and definitely not saggy either...

Well, she was engineered as a homunculus-like creature, right? No point competing against those marvelous melons. For some reason, I could sense a darkness brewing from behind the gazes of Yumina, Lu, Sue, and Elze. Sakura didn't seem to care all that much, and Leen was old enough to realize she wasn't going to grow anymore. Yae kept hers pressed down with a chest wrap, but her goods were top-tier. Hilde's chest was of a fair size, as well.

"I wonder if Flora's using some kind of drug to enhance her chest..."

"Nah, the chest-booster drug is in the storehouse, so she was probably just created...that...way..."

I replied to Linze too quickly to realize my mistake. And thanks to that, I suddenly found several gazes boring into me. I'd said something I shouldn't have.

"What did you say just now, Touya?"

"...Chest-booster drug?"

"It's in the storehouse, is it? Hm? You mean there's actually something like that?"

"Touya? Touya? Answer us, Touya."

"N-No! Wait! I just made a mistake!"

Please stop glaring at me! It's scary! At least blink! C'mon! Think about it! That's something Doctor Babylon made! It's obviously gonna have terrible side effects! It'll make your boobs balloon out to over three hundred centimeters or something! There'll definitely be something wrong with it!

"Elze, Lu. Head to the research laboratory and bring Doctor Babylon. We need more information about this drug. Linze and I will head to the storehouse and procure the substance."

"Roger!"

"On our way!"

On Yumina's order, Elze and Lu rushed off to the research laboratory.

How're you guys moving that fast?!

"We'll be off, then."

"Indeed."

Yumina and Linze dashed off toward the storehouse.

Wait, are you guys using [Accel] from your engagement rings?!

"That sounds kinda interesting. I'll check it out too!"

"Mhm… Me too…"

Sue and Sakura dashed off to the storehouse after the other two.

"I must admit, I'm a bit curious about this as well."

"Indeed, I am most interested, I am."

"Quite."

Leen, Yae, and Hilde stood up and ran off as well.

"…Why couldn't I have kept my fat mouth shut?"

At the very least, they were going to ask Doctor Babylon about it. I wanted them to be aware of any side effects, since I was certain there'd be some.

After a short while, I found out that Doctor Babylon had explained the full nature of the chest-booster drug to the girls.

Apparently, it induced a form of physical alteration, which acted as a supplement to change the shape of a body using magic. It also had to be applied directly to the chest.

I didn't get to see it in action, but all the girls tried it and their breasts actually did get bigger. However, the effect wasn't permanent. It sapped the person's personal magical supply to maintain itself, so over time, the breasts would slowly deflate to their original size. Surprisingly, there weren't actually any side effects. That was the most shocking part to me.

It only lasted around thirty or so minutes... I was just glad there was no loose skin or sagging afterward. Their chests were simply back to how they were before they'd used the drug. And since the drug made use of a person's own internal magic, I couldn't just use [**Transfer**] to keep it steadily sated.

Elze and Linze, who hadn't yet awakened to their beneficiary trait, began praying for theirs to be a deeper magic supply. Still, no matter how big the pool, it'd run out eventually. It was basically like constantly firing off a [**Fireball**] spell.

It was an ephemeral, transient thing, like a dream. It was fated to fade away, leaving nothingness in its wake...

Doc Babylon came over to me a little while after and told me she had a male version as well. I didn't really understand why a man would want a bigger chest, so she went on to explain that the male version didn't enlarge the chest...

"Phoenix down, tears of a Holy Dragon, a saintly white snake's molt, and a Unicorn horn…"

"Ayup. Gotta mix 'em into fertilizer. Our enemy slowly took divine venom inta his body, aye? Well, we'll grow ourselves a puretree that slowly absorbs divine stuff inta itself…" Uncle Kousuke nodded as he spoke, glancing at a twenty-centimeter sapling in the nearby soil every now and then.

"We gotta let it take in the holy essence've purebeasts. We divine folk're much too powerful, so we gotta use less strong stuff in the mix, basically. Yer heavenly beast friends are a bit too strong too."

"Sounds like it's tough to balance…" If we gave the tree too much divinity, it'd basically be like a benefactor of the gods. And then, it would just get killed by the divine venom instead of being able to purify it.

All the raw materials that had been requested were ones with purifying properties. Phoenixes constantly resurrected themselves, and Unicorns were said to have healing powers. If our puretree took in aspects like that, it'd be pretty good.

But the fact that we needed purebeasts was a problem…

They weren't magical beasts or anything like that, which meant that they weren't predators or threats to humans. They were reasonably intelligent and could communicate with people as well.

So basically, we couldn't just go kill them and be done with it. We had to negotiate to get them to willingly give up their aspects.

"The Holy Dragon, saintly white snake, and the Phoenix should be fine. Luli has a Holy Dragon among her subordinates… The snake should be easy if we use Sango and Kokuyou, and the Phoenix will be easy if we ask Kougyoku to talk to one, as well. The only issue is the Unicorn."

"Well…what about Kohaku, then? Purebeast's still a beast, aye? Can't she ask?"

"Apparently, Kohaku doesn't really like Unicorns… They'll just fight if they end up meeting each other… She seems to have a personal problem with them."

"Mm… It'd be plenty bad if we killed a Unicorn. Its lingerin' regret an' negative emotions would seep into the horn, which would make it pointless ta even bother gettin'."

Unicorns apparently lived in a sacred grove within the Sea of Trees. It was a place cut off from the outside world, a place that couldn't easily be accessed. I didn't think that was much of an issue for me, though. I had a good relationship with the Rauli tribe, which was the current dominant tribe over there.

The only real problem was that Unicorns didn't allow men near them. They allegedly only let pure maidens approach…which meant even if you were a girl, you had to be a virgin to get within a meter of one.

From what I'd heard, Unicorns were ferocious and cruel creatures. If a man or a sexually experienced woman approached one, they'd mercilessly aim to kill. If they were captured or bested, they'd rot their own horn and kill themselves… I couldn't really understand that mindset, myself.

They certainly seemed like a giant pain in the ass.

"I'll try to get a horn."

"Aye. I'll leave that to ya, then. Once ya gather the ingredients, we'll make us a fine puretree ta purify the divine venom."

…Well. I'm definitely gonna need help here… Hopefully, the girls are up for it.

"A Unicorn, you say?"

"…So a womanizing horse? Sounds like a real freak. But we can handle it."

...That's kinda harsh, Elze... You're not making it sound like a very pure creature at all.

Hunting the Unicorn wouldn't yield the horn we wanted, so I decided that negotiation was the best course of action. Since it'd be hostile toward men or non-virgin women, I figured I'd need to recruit a couple of virgins to help out.

Don't worry, though. I had enough tact that I didn't go up to my fiancees and say something stupid like, "You're definitely all virgins, right?" I just told them that bringing several girls might make the Unicorn feel more at ease.

I took all my fiancees and moved to the Sea of Trees. The Rauli tribe was currently the tribe of the treelord, making them the head honchos. I had permission from their matriarch, Pam, to enter the Unicorn grove.

"Are you sure we can talk to the Unicorns?"

"Kohaku said it should be all right. Purebeasts are intelligent creatures, and they know human language," I quickly answered Hilde. To be honest, the intellectual capacity these Unicorns had kind of made them annoying, since it meant they could subscribe to weird moral outlooks like prioritizing virgins.

"I've spoken with Unicorns before... They're rather strange creatures. Very knightly and gentle with virgin women, they even say 'milady' and such. But if a Unicorn senses a sexually experienced woman, everything changes. It'll swear violently at her, call her all manner of names, and try to shun her."

"What?" I wasn't really happy hearing that from Leen. But man, if it treated women so horribly, I was kind of worried how it might feel about a guy like me.

"...How do they determine if a girl's a virgin or not?"

"Dunno... They probably smell it?"

"I think I'm gonna be sick..." Lu shuddered slightly as she listened to Sakura and Linze talk.

Smell... Does that mean it's pheromone-based or something? But if it judges your purity based on smelling you... Ugh, that's kinda gross.

"Oh, Touya! Look over there. It's a pretty spring."

We headed deeper into the grove and found an open area and a spring. The crystal-clear waters and pools reminded me of the cenotes found at the Yucatan Peninsula.

"Touya... Look over there." Yumina pointed forward, and I saw a Unicorn drinking from the waters.

"A Unicorn..."

It basically looked like a white horse. Still, the beautiful white horn was a dead giveaway as to its pure nature. We had to get it.

"I probably shouldn't get any closer."

"You're right. It's already taken notice of you. I'm assuming the only reason it hasn't attacked is because it can't tell how strong you are." Leen pointed out the fact that the Unicorn had stopped drinking. It was staring right at us.

Wh-What's with those eyes?! It kind of feels like I'm being sized up by a thug!

"Tch..."

Did... Did it just click its tongue at me?! It did! Can Unicorns even do that?! What the hell?!

"It is not quite the creature I expected, it is not..."

"Mhm...it kind of has a bad vibe?" Yae and Hilde glanced nervously at each other.

"I guess not all Unicorns are friendly, huh? Who should approach it?"

"I-I feel a tad awkward, I do. Perhaps Lu-dono should go first..."

"M-Me?!"

"Oh, sounds like the best idea to me. You're a princess, and you're kinda meek!" Elze and Yae patted Lu on the back, sending her off for the first try.

Lu slowly, but surely, approached the Unicorn. The Unicorn kept its eyes trained on Lu. It kept on glaring at her, a faint expression of disgust on its face.

"G-Good day to you, Unicorn. My name is Lucia. I'd like to—"

The Unicorn simply turned away from Lu's smiling face.

...*Why's it being like that?* Lu circled around to face the Unicorn, and it just turned away again. No matter how she moved, the Unicorn moved to avoid looking at her.

"E-Excuse me."

"Keep away from me."

The Unicorn sounded disgusted. Its words confused all of us. Unicorns were supposed to react warmly to virgin maidens, so for it to reject Lu...

"H-Hold on! Don't go jumping to conclusions!" Lu came charging back toward us. She had small tears in her eyes and looked completely shocked.

"I-I'm a virgin, I swear! I wouldn't even dream of doing it with someone other than Touya! Believe me, please!"

"I-I know, Lu... It's okay. Just calm down, okay?"

It's pretty obvious she's a virgin. I certainly haven't done anything with her yet. She's kind of scaring me with how frantic she looks, though.

"...What does this mean, then?"

I was gently patting Lu on the head when Yumina spoke up.

"Y-Yumina! Please don't tell me you doubt me!"

"No, that's not what I mean. It's clear you're a chaste maiden, so I don't understand why the Unicorn's avoiding you."

Yeah, that's right. The Unicorn's clearly the weirdo here... Poor Lu.

"Maybe he has a type? Perhaps we should try sending out someone who's the exact opposite of Lu... Yae, you should go this time."

"Leen-dono... I am not sure what to make of what you just said, I am not..." Yae sighed and trudged off toward the Unicorn. But, when she reached out to touch it, the Unicorn backed off as if being approached by a pile of trash.

Yae scowled and reached forward again, but the Unicorn jumped back and yelled, "Don't touch me! You stink of man!"

"Th-That is not the case, it is not!" Yae screamed as she charged back toward me with tears in her eyes. Just like Lu, she tackled me and held on to my side.

"I-I would never consort with other men, I would not!"

"I know, Yae... I know. I think it's talking about me."

The Unicorn seemed to hate having any trace of a man near it, which was a huge problem.

We still needed its horn.

"I'll try next…"

"Sakura? You sure?"

"It's okay… Don't really care what it says to me. I'll just tell it what we need…" Sakura quietly hummed to herself as she walked up to the Unicorn. It seemed interested in her tune, and it wasn't trying to get away like it had been earlier. Unlike Yae and Lu, Sakura kept some distance while she was singing. And when she finished her song, she spoke up.

"We need your horn… Give it to us…"

"Gwuh… I thought a nice chick showed up, but you're just another gold-digging hussy? Bite me, bitch. You just wanna give it to your boyfriend and leave me on my own, don't you?"

Unicorn horns were a powerful restorative drug when crushed up into a powder. That meant historically, the horns have sold for high prices. It wasn't too unreasonable for the Unicorn to assume we'd come with that kind of intention.

But that Unicorn was definitely starting to piss me the hell off. I didn't care who it was, it had no right to speak to Sakura that way. Just who did it think it was messing with?

"I think we should kill this foolish horse, I do. If I sliced through its neck before it feels negativity, the horn should remain pure, it should," Yae scowled and muttered, echoing my own thoughts.

I didn't really want to kill it, though… Or at the very least, I would rather have saved killing for the last resort.

"I think we need to change our approach. Right now, we're simply asking the Unicorn for its horn, right?"

"Right, so what do you propose?"

"We just need to make the Unicorn ask us to take its horn."

Clearly we were getting nowhere, so we just needed to take the horn while the Unicorn felt good. *Heheheh... You pathetic horse... I'm gonna send you to heaven in more ways than one...*

"Your face is quite menacing, it is."

"He's already thought of something cruel, I can feel it."

I ignored Yae and Elze and moved forward. After calling Sakura back, I approached the Unicorn. Its gaze was no longer thuggish. Instead, it was staring through me with pure hatred in its eyes.

"Seems you don't really like guys, huh?"

"Huh? Don't talk to me, normie. I hate bastards like you the most. You just pick up chicks left and right, like you're some kind of alpha or some shit. But then you don't even bang them, so what's the point? You think you're so high and mighty 'cause you can resist a man's natural urges? Who gives a shit? How about you go to hell and let some other guys have a turn, huh?!"

After hearing that, I was honestly concerned that we wouldn't be able to use his horn for the puretree. His mindset was so corrupted that it felt like a lost cause. I sighed and shrugged, resigning myself to my initial plan.

"[Prison]."

"The hell?!"

I set up a barrier around two meters in diameter around the Unicorn. It wouldn't be able to escape.

"Hey, fucko! Let me out! This isn't funny! You want my horn to fall off?! I'll kill myself to spite you!"

"Calm down, dude. I'm just gonna call a few ladies who wanna spend some quality time with you."

"You serious?!"

"[**Rise forth, O Spirits!**]! Come to me!" Three beautiful girls appeared within the [**Prison**]. They'd taken the form of impeccably gorgeous teens. The three of them fluttered their eyelashes at the Unicorn.

"Oooh!"

The Unicorn let out a happy noise. I hoped the perverted bastard enjoyed it while he still could.

"Here, I'll call some more out. Just for you."

Several different beauties appeared out of thin air inside the [**Prison**]. One of the girls pushed down on the Unicorn's neck, causing him to lie down. The other girls flocked around him and pressed their bodies against him.

"Ohoho, now this is what I'm talking about! You don't stink like guys, you're totally virgins! This is what I deserve! Hahaha! About time!"

More and more spirits appeared, leaving the Unicorn in the middle of them all. He was smiling wide and looked extremely happy. I took that chance to begin negotiations with the purebeast.

"So, how about it? I'll let you have a whole day of fun with these girls if you give me your horn."

"Huh? Just one day? I want three. Give me three days, or get the hell outta here."

"Psh… You drive a hard bargain, man. But sure, three days it is. Give me the horn up-front, and I promise I'll keep my end of the deal."

I tweaked the [**Prison**] to only allow the Unicorn's horn to pass through. Then, I used Brunhild to cleanly slice it off. Because the Unicorn presented its horn to me of its own volition, there wasn't a single bit of impurity residing within it.

"Better hold up your end, bud. I don't want these hotties vanishing or anything."

"No worries, the spirits are gonna stay in there with you for three whole days. Hear that, spirits? You can return to your regular forms now if you want."

The spirits all smiled and cheered, their bodies morphing slightly as they spoke.

"Huh?"

The Unicorn let out a confused response because the pretty young ladies surrounding him sounded a touch...masculine.

The maidens began to transform into beefy old men and shredded young guys, one after the other. The Unicorn stared in shock and horror as the bodybuilder-esque forms materialized all around him. It was a veritable sausage party.

"Wh-Wh-What the hell is going on?!"

What was going on? That was simple. These spirits were all related to the most rugged and manly spirit around, the Stone Spirit. They all had chiseled forms that corresponded to minerals and ores. They were the pinnacle of manly musculature.

They didn't smell like men because spirits had no scents to begin with. I'd used my authority to call them into this world, and I'd shaped their forms as I'd done so.

"I'll be sure to send in some booze, snacks, and other bits and pieces. I hope you boys get along. Make it real close and personal. I'm sure you'll enjoy it."

I transported a few casks of ale into the [Prison], along with some food. It was gonna be a three-day beefy bonanza in there, after all. The spirits all cheered, celebrating and reveling in their party. Meanwhile, the Unicorn was huddled up in the corner, weeping and dribbling snot. At least now it looked as pathetic as its personality.

"I-I'm fine with you breaking our promise, s-so just let me out! I don't want this! Auugh! Th-They're too muscley! It's gross! They're all sweaty!"

"Ahaha, don't be so coy. You asked for three days, remember? I'll leave you to the fun."

"N-No! Please! Th-The beefcakes! They're… Their hands, oh god! What are they gripping?! D-Don't touch that!"

"Have fun, pal."

I turned around and left the area, refusing to look back. Yumina and the other girls were staring at me kind of funny, but I got the horn, and that was all that really mattered.

A while later, I heard from Pam that the Rauli tribe had spotted a peculiar Unicorn that refused to approach women. But apparently, it was quite fond of beefy young men…

It seemed the Unicorn had been compensating for something, and in a way…it had found its own happiness in life.

I just pretended not to know a thing.

"Mhm. S'all good here. The puretree's workin' about as well as we'd thought. Now any divine venom'll get turned into harmless mana," Uncle Kousuke, the god of agriculture, gave me the good news. His words prompted me to cheer.

"Hell yeah!"

The tiny sapling had taken in all the purifying elements we'd gathered, and used them to successfully turn into a budding puretree.

"So now we can start purifying all the venom in Isengard. And after that…"

"Mhm. We'll be able to face the wicked god directly," I said as I nodded at Yumina.

"But won't a little sapling like this take forever to purify such a large landmass like Isengard?" Sue, who was sitting near Anubis, raised a valid question.

"Won't be a problem at all, little lady. It turns the divine venom into mana, aye? Then it uses that mana to nourish itself. The moment we plant it in Isengard, it should start growin' an' growin'. The bigger it gets, the more it'll absorb, and the more it'll grow. But uh, well…" Kousuke smiled softly and turned toward her as he said that.

"What is it? There a problem?"

"Nah, s'just… Speakin' the obvious here, but it'd be better ta plant the sapling in the middle'f the country. But it ain't like we or yer wives-ta-be can go there due to the venom… Sure, we could send Anubis an' Bastet, but that's not really ideal either…"

Huh, why not? The capital of Isengard, Isenberg, is way to the south. We don't need to go someplace that dangerous, since the plant just needs to get placed in the central area. Anubis and Bastet can get there pretty easily, so what's the problem?

"Well, if Anubis an' Bastet plant the puretree in the middle'f Isengard…it'll start absorbin' the venom an' growin' bigger, right? It'll purify the land, but it'll get bigger an' bigger."

"Isn't that what we want?"

"D'ya really think the enemy's gonna leave it alone once they notice?"

"Oh, right…"

Duh. They're not morons. The puretree's a huge thorn in their side, so there's no way they'd leave it be. They'll definitely try and take it out the moment they realize it's there.

"Anubis an' Bastet are both scouting Gollems. They ain't built for offense, so there's no way they can protect the puretree."

"Yeah, we couldn't do that at all! If Sis and I got attacked by the wicked god's forces, we'd be scrap metal!" Anubis spoke in a lively fashion, but didn't raise his head from the floor. That posed an issue, for sure.

"So we need to figure out how to keep the tree safe until it reaches Isenberg... Can't we just plant it in the city directly?"

"Can't do that, Your Highness! There's a bunch of really scary Skeletons that'd rush into the city and chop it to bits!" Anubis declined my suggestion as he sniffed around the sapling.

Tsk... I can't believe that dumb mutt actually shot my plan down. Still, I guess he's right. That golden palace was surrounded by Skeletons, last I heard. They'd definitely wipe out the sapling before it gets big enough.

"I guess it'd be best to plant it a good distance away from our foes, then defend it while it slowly purifies more territory. We'll need a team, though."

"Hold on, Touya... Won't whoever goes have to guard that thing all day?" Sue said as she pouted a bit. I understood why she found the idea unappealing. Spending a whole day fighting non-stop to defend a tree wasn't exactly anyone's idea of a good time.

"A guard rotation would probably be best..."

"Don't think ya gotta worry about a rota. Once the venom around the saplin' is purified, we can send in Moroha, Karina, an' Takeru to guard the place."

Yeah, fair enough. Once the sapling's been there a little while, we can stay around it without worrying about the venom. I can't imagine Moroha and the others losing against whatever the wicked god sends, so we should be sorted... Still, I can't help but imagine Moroha accidentally slicing the tree in half, or Takeru putting a fist-shaped hole through it or something... I should ask Karina to keep an extra close eye on them.

"Once the purification reaches the enemy stronghold, y'can head down there yerself as well. After that, jus' drag out the wicked god an' beat it to a pulp."

I didn't think it'd go quite that smoothly, but we'd basically prepared for it as much as possible.

"Should we plant the puretree now, then?"

"It'd be better to wait a bit jus' ta make sure we got the kinks ironed out. Don't want any weird side effects or nothin'."

That made sense. We didn't want anything bad to happen after the sapling was planted, since Uncle Kousuke couldn't just walk over into the venom and sort it out. The plan was set. Once everything was in place, the sapling would go into the [Storage] on Anubis' collar, and he'd go out to Isengard with Bastet.

"Should I send Albus over as well, Touya?"

"Sounds good. We should give them a little defense so they can hold out until I get a [Gate] set up or something."

I'd have Anubis take a [Gate] mirror we could pass through, and we would head over once the purification had been going on for a little bit. After that, I'd call on some Frame Gears. The best place for the puretree to be planted was a forest. That way, it'd basically be hiding in plain sight, which would prevent the enemy from finding us out as easily.

We left Kousuke behind while he worked out the last details of the puretree, then headed out of the greenhouse.

"Looks like we can finally go on the offensive."

"Well, we have to defend the puretree first," I sighed quietly in response to Yumina. We had to defend before we could attack. It was a bit funny to think about it that way.

"And then we're gonna get married! Let's pull out all the stops!"

"Relax a little, Sue… I dunno if I wanna make it a flashy affair…"

"No way! We gotta! It's a once-in-a-lifetime experience! We'll need to line the streets with a festival and stuff! If we don't now, then when else could we?!"

I understood what Sue meant, but still… Well, I wasn't the one planning the wedding stuff anyway, so that was out of my hands.

It was a wedding that involved four princesses: Yumina, Lu, Hilde, and (illegitimately) Sakura. There was no way it'd be a quiet affair. My cousin once told me that the man was basically a piece of decoration during a wedding, and it'd be better to just let the woman do as she pleased. Though in this case, it'd be a lot of women…

Yumina and Sue happily chatted about the wedding as we walked back to the castle. After a short while, they both pulled out their smartphones and started flicking across their screens.

"Something up?"

"Software update… Looks like a few new apps got released."

"Oh, yeah. If I remember right, the new apps should be the Levitation app, the Speaker app, and Lu's Cooking Blog app."

The mass-produced smartphones regularly received software updates from Babylon. The apps on these phones were magical and were distributed via [Enchant] and [Program]. They allowed the use of certain spells, even if the wielder of the phone didn't have the aptitude for it. The magic power for the apps would still have to come from the individual's mana stores, though.

The Levitation app was handy for carrying heavy stuff (though you couldn't lift it higher than your head) and the Speaker app was useful for any world leaders who needed to give out speeches or commands to their citizens.

The leaders of the western continent were especially excited by these apps, since much fewer people on that side of the world could use magic. Obviously, it was just basic utility stuff. We didn't want to install any dangerous software on their phones or anything.

The Cooking Blog app was basically just a blog that Lu had set up to share recipes and her commentary on them. It had taken a little while to start, but I was glad it had finally made its debut.

The app didn't have too many recipes on it just yet, though. Just a few simple dishes and desserts. Lu planned to add a few recipes each week, and she also wanted to showcase meals from countries other than Brunhild. It kind of seemed like it'd become less of a cooking blog and more of a world food tour blog.

Well, whatever the case, it was good that the apps were going down well with everyone. The Weather app was one of our most popular ones, actually. The app gave the temperature averages for the day, when the sun would rise and set, and various information about what kind of weather to expect that day. It was pretty useful for world leaders. They could use it to send out weather warnings, and also prepare for potential natural disasters. A few rainmakers and shamans who claimed to be able to call the rain ended up losing their jobs as a result, though.

The weather in this world was mostly managed by the spirits, and I happened to have mastery over those spirits. Therefore, there was nothing wrong with me exercising that power to make the weather whatever I wanted it to be... Though it was kind of a pain, so I didn't interfere regularly or anything. The smaller weather spirits were kind of like preschoolers, so it was hard to herd them. Plus, sometimes they didn't listen to me... They really felt like unruly kids.

I left Yumina and Sue at the castle and headed up to Babylon's research laboratory.

Apparently, Doc Babylon had come up with a new invention after watching a mecha anime. I was hoping it was something that could make our Frame Gears fly.

"Hey, Doc, heard you'd completed a new invention?"

"Heheheh... That's right, Touya! Behold the fruits of my labor, the inspired creation I came up with after viewing the culture of your world!" Atlantica...or rather, Tica...suddenly brought over a small box-shaped object. It had been a while since I'd seen her, even though she served as the doc's assistant and the research laboratory's manager. The box piqued my interest, though. I took it into my hands. It was clearly cardboard, and it had an illustration on the front. It depicted a Knight Baron standing atop a fallen behemoth. I flipped the box to the underside, but there wasn't anything drawn there. It was just a rough cardboard surface.

I opened the box up to check the contents. There were several plastic pieces held together by frames that you could just pop out and start assembling. They'd even had the foresight to include an instruction manual!

I knew exactly what this was. However, I still decided to ask Doc Babylon, just to be sure.

"…What am I looking at, here?"

"It's a plastic model, duh!"

"…And this is the invention you had me so excited about?!" I screamed and scowled at the doctor, but she just flashed a thumbs-up.

It's pretty amazing that they managed to make a scale model after seeing an anime with them, but this isn't really helpful at all!

I was honestly pretty amazed. Despite it being a 1/144 scale model, it was fully articulated and the cockpit hatch could open!

"It's made out of a resin-like material we've infused with ether liquid. It doesn't require glue. The parts just stick to each other with magic magnetism. It's pretty much indestructible too. Even if it got crushed by a carriage, it'd remain intact. It's the strongest scale model in the world, muahaha!"

"Why the hell did you do that?!"

What kind of scale model is this, exactly…? Geez.

"It doesn't end there, my friend. Check this out."

Doc Babylon picked up the knight baron and set it atop a mithril circle on the table. Then, a little panel appeared on the circle, which she placed her hand on. At that instant, I felt magic course through the metal surface.

The Knight Baron on the table started to move. It raised its shield into the air, then drew its sword. And after that, it swung its weapon a few times, gracefully waltzed around the surface, and returned to its original pose. That was pretty impressive...

"How about them apples? We combined magic particle field resonance with localized magic synchronization, and— Oww! Stop, oww!"

"...This is what you've been dedicating so much time to making?! This is what you've been holed up working on?!"

I mercilessly pinched the tiny doctor's cheeks, not caring for her previously proud expression. The idiot had decided making toys was a noble pursuit while we were all trying our best to counteract the wicked god!

"Ahh... A man bullying a little girl... Mmh... Ah... That's so naughty... How subtly sadistic... Who knows what it could lead to, aaah!"

"Shut the hell up, you wannabe diddler!"

I glared daggers in Tica's direction. I knew it wouldn't take long for that degenerate to start showing her true nature.

"Nyooooh... Waith, waith! I didnh't jusht make thihs to playyhhh!" Doctor Babylon cried out as I smooshed her cheeks. I let go of her, and Tica brought over a small disc-like device with wings. It vaguely resembled a flat airplane. I would've appreciated it more if she hadn't been breathing so heavily and rubbing her thighs together, though...

Doc Babylon put the small device under the Knight Baron's feet... It was kind of like a surfboard.

Oh... Maybe she did consider the flying unit, after all.

"I thought about a flight module that attached to the back, but that would have limited the Frame Gears it could be attached to. That's why I came up with this model. There are hooks that dig into the feet to keep it stable. I call it the flight gear."

The Knight Baron floated upward slightly thanks to the flight gear underneath it. It was interesting seeing it in action. It did a little loop, floating around and swerving a bit before the miniature jumped down off it to the table's surface. Then, the flight gear folded its wings inward and fell, the Knight Baron caught it and held it up... It had transformed into a hefty shield.

"So we can use it for defense as well?"

"Sure can. The bottom is reinforced with extra-hard phrasium. I'd say it can hold off plenty of attacks... Probably not a particle beam blast, though."

It was smart of her to coat the bottom of the flight gear with phrasium, since it reduced the chances of us being shot down by anti-air measures.

"The only issue is that the flight gear saps magic at a very rapid pace, and it's a bit difficult to maneuver. Unfortunately, in its current state, it's not really usable by any of our pilots... On top of that, it can't reach an especially high altitude, so you can forget about flying among the clouds... Oh, right. Yumina and Leen probably shouldn't bother using it, either. It'll definitely move too erratically for their ranged attacks to be useful."

I guess it was more accurate to call it something that facilitated floating, rather than flying. It allowed for good speed, at least. Honestly, it was probably more useful for commanders to float above the battlefield and get a good grasp of the situation.

"I've been using the plastic model as a small-scale simulation, but I'm planning to make a full-size test model soon."

"...Well, I'm just glad you didn't make a scale model for no reason."

"No reason?! Perish the thought, Touya! This model represents the budding genius that we can inspire in children! I want to make this, I want to build this, I want to change this! We need to show children that science is power, Touya! We need them to just do it! They can't let their dreams be dreams! They need to make it a shining reality! I have unearthed the multidimensional treasure known as scale models, and I have transposed it unto this world! With this, a whole new generation may be inspired!" Doc Babylon started spouting gibberish as she balled up her fists and went red in the face. My gaze on her just grew colder. I wasn't buying her story at all. She hadn't made the scale model to inspire kids, she'd just done it because she wanted to... Still, it was a pretty well-made item... It'd definitely sell well in Olba's store.

Hmm... Models from a certain series are called gunpla in my world, but that doesn't really fly here... Maybe the ones based on Frame Gears should be called frampla? Gearpla? Well, who knows... It's not like they need to have a particular brand name. Anyone could make these with molds and ether liquid resin, anyway.

In the days to come, little plastic models of our Frame Gears became the iconic souvenir people bought upon visiting our country. I wasn't really sure how to feel about scale models of robots being a national staple of Brunhild, but it was beyond my control.

"Gotta admit, it's surprising."

"Yeah, it sure is. His divinity's actually getting purer than ours at this point... He'll probably end up having a deeper well of it too.

Guess that's what happens when God Almighty himself takes an interest in you."

Karina, Moroha, and I were in the middle of a forest. More specifically, we were in the middle of a [**Prison**] I had set up within the forest. I'd just activated my apotheosis and unleashed all the divinity I could. I could feel the power coursing through me, and there were even white particles of light flitting from my body. To be honest, going into that state made me feel on edge. It was like my body wanted to run rampant and unleash all of its power.

According to Uncle Kousuke, that was because my mind still hadn't caught up to my body in terms of divinity. Basically, my thoughts were still immature and more mortal-minded...

"Oh, your hair grew out again."

My platinum-blond hair, which was even whiter this time, flopped past my shoulders. That was strange, since I hadn't experienced hair growth like this since my fight against Gila.

"Looks like your divinity increased. More than you can control, again. It means your body's getting closer and closer to true godhood. Honestly, the most amazing thing about you is how you can turn it on and off. Going from mortal to god at the push of a button. It's kind of a harder process for us to become human."

"Well...it's not like I'm becoming human, right? I started off as one."

"Oh... That might be it, yeah. Your body isn't really human at this point, but you're definitely a human soul residing in the body of a god. Given that state of being, it's not to so surprising that you can enter both human and godly states on a whim."

My body had been accidentally constructed with materials from the divine realm. Or, more specifically, it was a body formed of God Almighty's divinity. That would technically make me something like a blood relative to the old man, apparently.

"I just wanted to be sure of the state of your divinity before we faced off against the wicked god, but it looks like there's nothing to worry about. You just need to make sure not to screw up. Don't be careless."

"Ahahaha, yeah! You can't take after God Almighty that closely, you know? Being careless is his special talent!"

"Pffft, you got that right, Sis!"

Karina and Moroha laughed alongside each other. I, on the other hand, was not laughing... Why? Because I saw who had appeared behind them prior to their comments.

"Ahem! Did someone call for the god of carelessness...?" God Almighty cleared his throat, making my two foolish sisters straighten up immediately.

"Wh-Wh-What are you doing here, sir?"

"Well, I decided to take a little bit of leisure time. It has been a while since I last saw you all, after all. I must admit, I am quite surprised to be the subject of your comment, though."

He wore a soft smile, but his eyes were like that of a hawk. Moroha and Karina both started sweating profusely. I'd certainly never seen them like this before. It was pretty interesting, to be honest.

"O-Oh, geez! Look at the time! I have an appointment at the training field! Better get to it, see ya!"

"Wh... Wait! Um... Err... Oh yeah, Crea asked me to go hunt down two, uh...no, three wild birds for her! I'm super busy! Better get hunting! Bye!"

The two of them sputtered terrible excuses and vanished into thin air. They had fled.

"Goodness, those girls... They certainly treat things rather lackadaisically, do they not? I do hope they have not caused you any bother."

"Ahaha... Well, they help me out a lot, so it pretty much evens out."

I reversed my apotheosis and returned to human form. It definitely felt like pressing a switch, just how Moroha described it. Unfortunately, my hair was still past my shoulders.

"It has been a while, my lad. How have you been?"

"Not bad, thanks. Is it all right for you to be down here?"

"Oh, it is no matter at all, sonny. This body is simply a clone-like extension of my real self. The real me is back up in the divine realm, taking care of business. Thus, there are no problems at all."

A clone, huh...? Kinda like when he used that avatar to come down last time? That's pretty nifty. Wonder if I'll be able to replicate myself like that.

"I think we should probably head back to the castle. I'd rather talk to you in a comfier environment."

"A wise idea. It has been some time since I last met with your young ladyfriends, after all."

I opened up a [Gate] and took God Almighty back to the castle.

Back when he first came to the world, he introduced himself as my grandfather, Mochizuki Shinnosuke. The castle staff believed this to be his identity and treated him as they would any other royal. My fiancees, on the other hand... Well, it was a bit different there. Since they were aware he was the god of worlds, effectively God Almighty and the highest-ranking deity, they found it a little hard to interact with him.

"Now, now, my dears. You need not worry about my status. When I am here, I am but a simple grandfather. Nothing more, nothing less."

"O-Okay. Th-Then, welcome to our home, Grandfather."

"Indeed, that is good. You should call me that from now on," God Almighty said as he smiled at Yumina. I wondered if I should start calling him gramps or something.

He wanted to talk with me alone, so we headed out to the balcony after that short interaction.

"The reason for my visit is to check up on how the gods are spending their time and also to view the status of this new world. It is no longer within my jurisdiction, after all. Ordinarily, we would have the god of destruction come and remove it from the cycle or just let it wither away on its own, but I do hope that you can rise to the occasion and become its new caretaker."

"I just need to beat the wicked god first, right?"

"That is correct. So long as you remove that obstacle, this world will likely turn out well. You will save an entire world...or, well... two worlds from a grisly fate. I would be quite happy to have you as the caretaker here, though you might find some growing pains for the first one or two thousand years."

Apparently, I wouldn't be put in the caretaker position immediately after dealing with the wicked god. I'd spend a couple hundred years in the mortal world, while making occasional trips to the divine realm. I didn't exactly want to leave my family behind full-time, so this was the best compromise.

"There is a second reason I came down here, lad. After this world is secured under your protection and the wicked god is removed... I would like you to establish this place as a haven for the gods. In a sense, I would like this world to become a resort or vacation spot where gods could free themselves from their duties for a while. I will, of course, instate rules and such. I would not allow the gods to reveal their divinity, and they would have to be humans for the duration of their stay, things such as that."

"Wh… A resort?! I mean…I guess that's fair, there are a lot of gods here who are taking it easy as it is…"

I couldn't help but think of the freeloading gods in Brunhild… Yeah, they were definitely already using the place as a resort.

"Even gods need some time off now and then. I doubt they would be able to relax on a world under my watchful gaze, so this is the perfect spot. Though, I would not want them to relax too much…"

"Well…so long as they relax in moderation, I'm sure it'll be fine."

"That can be something we worry about later. I must say, this is rather good," God Almighty said as he sipped from a cup of green tea that Lu had poured for us both.

"How long do you think you'll be staying with us?"

"A few more days, if that does not impose. After that, I plan on traveling around the world to check on a few things."

Check on a few things? Geez… Well, I guess he can't really be hurt, so it should be fine.

"Oh wait, there's the situation in Isengard…"

"Ah yes, I know of it. That divine venom, yes? It is indeed lethal to the divine, but it does not affect gods of a higher echelon such as myself. It would not do a thing to me, so you need not worry."

"Huh?! But I heard that the more divinity you had, the stronger the effect…"

"Indeed, that is the case… But only for gods of a lower status. The divine venom was originally synthesized by accident, but its creator was a lower-ranked god of medicine. It certainly could not affect anyone with higher divinity than its original creator."

As a rule, gods that governed specific things were lower-ranked gods. Karen, the goddess of love, was an example of that. When a god ascended to a higher echelon, they took on multiple duties and traits, so it was no longer possible to refer to them as the "god of X" in a truly specific manner. Even God Almighty wasn't just the god of worlds. He was the god of all other kinds of things, like light and dark. Beginnings and ends. He probably had all kinds of divinity brewing inside of him.

"...So wait, you could probably just purify the venom, couldn't you?"

"Of course I could, my boy. I could do it in seconds. But what good would it be for you if your test examiner started filling in all the answers?"

"I guess you have a point..."

He was right. I shouldn't have even brought it up. Besides, Uncle Kousuke was offering plenty of support anyway... Frankly, I thought I was getting a little too much aid from that guy. Still...it wasn't exactly cheating. It was more like I was equipped with a top-of-the-line tutor to help me prep for my exams.

"Ohhh! It'sh true! God Almighty'sh here!"

A tiny drunken goblin shambled out from nowhere. It was the god of alcohol, Mochizuki Suika. She looked absolutely hammered.

"Oh, hello there. Are you well?"

"Hell, hic, yeah I am! Drinkin' aahhhll night. And drinkin' aaahhhll day! Hic! Lotsa booze down here!" Suika laughed, cackling in a shrill and generally unappealing manner. She was absolutely sloshed.

"Letsh have a little, hic, sip more... This one, hic, is from the mountainsh of Roadmareh... It'sh got a bit of a kick, hic! But it'sh shoo nice... Touyaaaa, bring me snacksh!!" Suika roared as she pulled a sake cup out of absolutely nowhere and started pouring alcohol into it, so I grabbed her by the nape of the neck and picked her up like a cat.

"You little twerp... Where'd you get this booze from, huh?"

"Hic! I, uhhm...went and shpoke to Audrey... Got shome booze in exchange for helping, hic, her kill some monsters... Eeehehehh..."

Audrey? Oh... Isn't that the name of the Doge of Roadmare?!
Did you seriously go all the way there just for something to drink?!
Ugh... I definitely owe the government of Roadmare an apology now,
don't I? What a hideous little gremlin you are...

Even in human form, a god was still a god. Suika was nowhere near Moroha or Takeru's level, but she was easily more than a match for some monsters.

"Hoh... This is indeed a good drink. Touya, do you perhaps have any snacks?"

"Wait...you're actually drinking? I mean, I do have some, but... Buh... Wait here..."

I brought edamame, sashimi, cold tofu, yakitori, and some other booze-appropriate snacks out to the balcony table.

"Don't eat too much, we have dinner later."

"Indeed, we shall not."

"Heeeh... In, hic, deed! Weee shahll noht."

God Almighty and Suika both raised their cups, and a sudden cheery tune began blowing in from nowhere. I knew the source right away, of course... It was Sousuke.

The melody was a certain song about drinking all year round and all the reasons to...

"Ooh. This looks fun, you know?"

"Aye, I'll say."

"Oh, nice to see you both."

Karen and Kousuke showed up. I really wished that they would learn to use the door, since their teleportation was a little annoying... It wasn't like I could do anything to stop them, but still! Moroha and Karina probably wouldn't dare come see God Almighty after what they'd said earlier and Takeru was training with Ende until nightfall, so at least there wouldn't be any more surprise visitors.

I decided to leave the gods to their own devices on the balcony as I headed back inside. But when I walked back into the room, I noticed Moroha and Karina quietly peeking out at the balcony. Those morons clearly wanted in on the festivities.

"I don't think he's actually mad. Just take these over, and I'm sure he'll forget about it."

I pulled out two high-grade Belfast wine bottles from [Storage], along with a fancy cheese board. Then, I passed them over to the girls.

"Oh… Thanks."

"What a good little bro you are!"

The two of them smiled and headed out to the balcony. Honestly…they were nothing but trouble.

"Hic! Ohh! Look, Karina and Moroha're heeere! Hic, wait! That'sh an amahzing wine! Lemme sip! Lemme sip!"

I could hear Suika's grating voice even though the doors were closed. I had a feeling dinner would probably end up being rowdy…

Well, whatever. I shrugged, then headed off to the kitchen so I could discuss the evening's menu with Crea.

"I'd appreciate it if you could handle that."

"Understood."

Albus, the white crown, sat atop the dog Gollem Anubis' back. Bastet, the cat Gollem, sat atop Albus' head. The three of them were headed off to plant the puretree within Isengard, which was supposed to purge the divine venom.

"...This might be a bit much. Anubis and Bastet don't stand out much because they're just a black cat and a black dog, but with Albus mixed in as well, it's... Hm..." Yumina said, letting out a small sigh as she looked over the trio.

"Yeah... But there's not really a lot we can do here. We definitely need Albus to protect the tree while it grows."

Anubis' [**Storage**] collar had the puretree sapling inside it, along with a large [**Gate**] mirror.

The sapling was to be placed somewhere covertly in Isengard, and Albus would defend it until the surrounding area had been purified. After that, we'd all be able to move in via the mirror. That was why Albus was necessary to the mission, but it was definitely true that he stood out a lot.

"Well, I don't think anyone'll bug you guys so long as nobody recognizes Albus as a crown."

"I will take care to move unnoticed."

Albus had a phrasium shortsword, just in case of trouble. He also had orders to abandon the sapling and return via the [Gate] mirror in the case of catastrophic failure. Worst case scenario, if the puretree sapling had to be left behind, we could nurture another one with the remaining purifying materials we had.

"Just try to avoid trouble. I'd prefer it if you stayed away from towns too. It'd be really bad if the enemy got wind of your presence based on rumors in the area."

"Understood. We'll be going."

"Indeed, let us go."

"Woof, woof! Let's gooo! Hold on tight, you two!" Anubis charged ahead, Albus clinging on to his collar for dear life, as the three Gollems hurtled through a [Gate] I'd opened.

I'd sent them to Gardio, along the coastline. They'd then cross the sea to Isengard from there. Assuming they went quickly, it'd take them about two days.

"It's in their hands now."

"They'll be okay. I believe in them…"

Yumina's words didn't have any real logical root, but hearing her say them made me believe it too. Everything was going to be okay, I just knew it.

"…You really are incredible, Yumina."

"Wh-What?"

My cute little fiancee, who seemed perplexed by the sudden compliment, tilted her head a bit to the side.

Everything was going to be okay. It was going to be fine. I held those beliefs firmly in my heart as I closed the [Gate] in front of me.

"Oho, this is quite the lively neighborhood," said God Almighty, smiling as he walked through the castle town.

"This is the main street, and then that's the road to Belfast. If you follow it in the other direction, you'll reach Regulus. The southern trail takes you to the guild area."

I was guiding him through Brunhild's main settlement. Ever since the guild had us link the town to the dungeon islands, there had been more and more people coming through on a regular basis. Merchants and adventurers alike came to the town. Some of them even decided they liked it enough to settle.

We had immigration screening, but it was pretty basic. We did a family background check and asked the individuals what kind of jobs they wanted to work, that sort of thing. Our main goal was to keep criminals out. That being said, we were happy to accept rehabilitated criminals. Luckily, Yumina's mystic eye helped us screen intentions pretty accurately. Plus, we had the polygraph test from Doc Babylon. We had to be wary of potential insurgents from Yulong and Sandora trying to take revenge on Brunhild's people, so better safe than sorry.

For the most part, the only criminals in Brunhild were foreigners, but there was the odd troublemaker here and there amongst our citizens. That was to be expected, though. A bigger population meant a bigger pool of potential problems.

"We're not a major city by any means, but we get by well enough."

"It is pleasant to see, all the same. I am happy to see such lively children running around," God Almighty said as he smiled over at a group of playful kids.

In this world, child labor wasn't an uncommon practice. The further out you got from the main cities, the more likely it was to find kids doing unskilled work. Education and manners weren't really a priority for the people who struggled just to eat, so they put their kids to work and pretty much quashed their potential.

But I wanted the children of Brunhild to grow up with freedom and opportunity, so that they could pursue their hopes and dreams.

"There's a school up ahead. Kids usually start attending from the age of six."

"Oh my."

I showed God Almighty to our elementary school. We didn't actually have any other tiers of school in the town, though. Sakura's mother, Fiana, was in charge of educating the townspeople.

Heh, looks like there's a lot of cats napping in the sunlight today. They sure like this schoolyard, huh? Hold on... Wait just a second... I noticed one particular cat curled up on a bench, so I immediately charged over to him and lifted him high.

"Are you slacking off over here?!"

"M-Meowie! I-I was just taking a catnap! We had a catnip party with Athos' friends and a bunch of ladycats yesterday, so, oh... A-Agh! G-Grand Duke, it's you?! Meow very n-nice to see you!" Mr. Mittens was half asleep, so he hadn't realized who had grabbed him as he said that. However, his fur stood up on end when he saw my face.

"Aren't you supposed to be looking after Fiana?"

"M-Meow... Er... M-My lady told me to rest for the day! I promise! Paw on heart!"

"Does Sakura know about this?"

"...Sh-She...doesn't..."

"Do you want me to call Kohaku so you can get a good earful?"

"Meooow! N-No! Spare me! I'll be a good kitty!" Mr. Mittens wailed and started bowing profusely. That dumbass really was something else.

"Ohohoh. What a funny little kitten this is."

"I'm no mere kitten! Meow very dare you!" Mr. Mittens hissed as he glared right up at God Almighty, staring him down with righteous fury.

"Oh, well… This is my grandpa. His name is Mochizuki Shinnosuke."

"A pleasure to meet you."

"Y-Your grandfather? Meow nice to meet you… My name is Mr. Mitt— D'Artagnan…"

Pfft… You almost called yourself Mr. Mittens, idiot.

"Oh? Our very own grand duke? Are you here to inspect the school?"

A window opened up nearby, and principal Fiana popped her head out. A series of other windows opened up in sequence, and children started peering outside as well.

"Grand Duke?"

"Ohh, it's the duke!"

"Play with us, mister!"

"Are you here to tell us more stories?"

The kids started murmuring amongst themselves. I felt a bit bad, since I'd clearly interrupted class. I apologized to Fiana, but took the chance to introduce God Almighty as my grandpa.

"Oh my, what a pleasant surprise. Welcome to our school. I hope it's to your liking."

"Oh, of course it is! Thank you so much for working alongside my grandson here. There are no difficulties you face while living in Brunhild, I hope?"

"None at all! The grand duke treats us all very well, and I'm more than happy with the children I teach," Fiana said as she smiled softly.

I was definitely happy to have her with us in Brunhild, and it was good for Sakura to be able to see her mother often as well.

Fiana lived in a small house close to the school with Mr. Mittens. I'd invited her to live alongside Sakura in the castle, but she turned the offer down. I had a feeling that she didn't want to live there because it would increase her chances of meeting with her ex-husband, the overlord.

God Almighty turned from Fiana to the children, and he ever-so-gently called out to them.

"Hello there, children! Are you enjoying school?"

"Yeah!"

"We wuv school!"

"I like school, but I don't like homework."

One of the children pouted a little bit, sounding unlike the rest of the crowd.

"Oho. Not one for studying, are you?"

"I'm gonna be a knight, so I don't gotta do classwork."

"Are you sure you can become a knight without classwork?"

"Yeah! I don't gotta have brains. Don't even gotta read! Just gotta be able to beat people up, right?"

The boy snorted slightly and picked at his nose as God Almighty looked him over. He was certainly a little bit bratty...

"Is that so, young man? Tell me, Grand Duke. What do you make of this?"

"Sorry, but you won't make it into our knight order that way."

"Huuuh?! But I thought I just had to be tough to save people!"

The boy complained loudly, almost throwing a little tantrum.

"Well then, tell me this: How many ration packs would a team of fifteen knights need if they were going out on a seven-day monster hunt? If they don't take enough, they'd end up being weakened, but if they take too much, they'll be carrying more than they should be and might be overburdened. If they fail the mission because of that, then the monsters would go on to hurt those people you want to save, right?"

"Wah…"

"If you found a bandit den and couldn't read the plans they'd left behind, they could attack a village while you were trying to figure out where they'd gone. I bet you'd wish you did your homework in a situation like that."

To be honest, he'd probably be fine if he was in a group, since someone else there could take care of the reading or calculating, but that wasn't really the point.

It was fine to do whatever if you were just a mercenary looking for cash. It was also fine if you were an adventurer going it alone out there. But if you were a member of a knight order, then you had a duty of care to the people you'd been assigned to protect.

One person making a mistake could have dire consequences. Those who believed physical strength was the only requirement weren't really the kind of people who had any business being knights. It was true that strength was important, but there were different kinds of strength. Mental acuity was certainly one of them.

"Our knight order has people who aren't all that physically strong too. We have a whole group dedicated to designing blueprints and helping grow more crops to make the land more sustainable. Those jobs help keep our citizens alive too. Physical strength will only get you so far."

Even I had to rely on Yumina and my other fiancees, along with Doc Babylon. Not to mention the monarchs and gods. I wouldn't have made it here without them… Even if they were a little annoying at times.

"...Really, miss?"

The boy turned toward Fiana, asking her for the truth. I felt a little sad that the kid didn't trust his own monarch at face value...

"It's true. Strength alone won't let you protect everything. You need to be strong in other areas, not just your body. That's why we have schools. It's my job to teach you, so that when you're an adult you can choose the path that's right for you."

The boy paused for a moment to process this new information, then gave a timid nod.

"...Okay! I'm gonna study real hard, miss! Gonna be a knight who can save people!"

"Good boy. I'm sure you'll do well."

The boy seemed to have a spark of determination in his eyes. I hoped that I'd see him again someday in the application line for Brunhild's knight order. God Almighty and I then talked with the kids a little more before turning and leaving the schoolyard.

"This is a pleasant country. Everyone seems to be quite energetic, and they are all working hard for their futures."

"There's still a lot about it that makes me think I need to grow as a leader, to be honest."

"Now, now. I will have you know that I have created many worlds since I came into existence. Some that turned out wonderfully, but others I have had accidentally destroyed. Some turned out to be vile places as well. Even a god such as myself cannot demand perfection from himself. You have allies to rely on, and I am sure they will be there for you."

I understood what he was saying, but the scale of his situation was unfathomably large. He was basically just telling me not to overexert myself, though.

"I have to ask, my boy. Do you regret being brought to this world? Is there a part of you that wishes to return home?"

"Well, I mean... When I first arrived here, I kind of treated the situation as something that couldn't really be avoided. It honestly hurts that I can't see my family anymore. I'm sad I can't see my old friends too. Sadder still that I'm dead to them. That's why I decided it was best to just make the most of the new life in this world. I've always been kind of good at making the best out of a bad situation. But now, I wouldn't call this situation bad at all. In fact, I'm happy to be here. I was able to meet a lot of people I hold close to my heart."

I'd met Elze and Linze not long after arriving in this world. Then, I traveled with Yae, met Sue quite by chance, and found myself close to Yumina...

I remember Leen offering to make me her student in Mismede, and then rescuing Lu during the Regulus coup... Oh, and I saved Hilde from the Phrase and restored Sakura's memories.

All of those events wouldn't have come to pass had I not died so suddenly, so I couldn't really regret it anymore.

"It would be possible for you to leave this world behind now that you have awakened to your divinity... You could simply use it to return home."

God Almighty had a point. Now that I'd become a god, I wasn't exactly beholden to the rules I'd been bound by as a mortal.

Still...I was formally dead back home. Suddenly coming back from the grave would have caused too much of a fuss. I wasn't all that interested in causing a media circus.

"I was kinda thinking that I'd introduce my fiancees to my parents by entering their dreams, or something. I don't think it'd be that weird for a parent to dream of their dead kid, right?

Plus, they're pretty open-minded in terms of beliefs, so I think they might be comforted by it."

My parents were a manga artist and a picture book illustrator, so they kind of had to have open minds to succeed. I had actually been keeping up with my dad's series on my smartphone. His manga wasn't selling great, but it hadn't been discontinued either, so that was a good sign.

"Ah, regarding your parents. Your mother is with child again. I just thought you ought to know. A little sibling of yours will soon be born into the world."

"Ohh, that's nice… Wait, what?!" I screamed. God Almighty had said that so casually it took a minute for my mind to process the news. A few people nearby jumped back in shock when I yelled, but I didn't care about that.

I-I'm getting a baby brother or sister?! Uhhh… My dad was twenty-four and my mother was eighteen when I was born… And when I died, they were forty and thirty-four…so…

I started to internally calculate how old my parents were.

"Guess I should try and appear in their dreams soon…"

I had to congratulate them, after all. I was happy to hear that they'd get another shot at happiness with a new child, but a part of me felt truly upset that I couldn't be there for my little sibling.

"I wonder if I should summon a dog or a cat beast to serve as a guardian for the little one… Or maybe I should summon a spirit that can't be seen… Yeah, a silent guardian might be better."

"Now, now, my boy. You are moving a little quickly there. The child has yet to be born, after all…"

"I'm gonna be a big brother! I've gotta make sure my little sibling's okay, and I want my family to be happy… Understand?"

"I will watch over the child, so fret not about any danger befalling your family. I see you are the type who loses his composure when family comes into the mix, eh?" God Almighty scolded me ever so slightly. He wasn't exactly wrong. I had a feeling that when I had kids, I'd be one of those oppressively doting dads. I worried for whoever ended up wanting to date my daughters, since I knew they'd have to contend with me.

Still, I had to admit...I felt a bit of relief when I learned my parents were having a baby. I was scared that they'd live a lonely life in that house after I was gone. My crazy grandpa passed away a while ago, so I had a feeling the little kid would probably grow up to be a decent and well-adjusted person... Unlike me.

I quietly stared up at the blue sky of this other world, praying for the wellbeing of the family I'd left behind in my original home.

"This location is suitable," Bastet said, then jumped down from atop Albus' head.

They were in an unnamed forest near the middle of Isengard. It was far from civilization, and not very notable at all.

"We're planting it here, then?"

"Indeed. Produce the sapling," Albus ordered.

Anubis did as he was told, and produced the puretree sapling from the [Storage] in his collar. It fell to the ground.

"Albus, the rest is up to you."

"Very well," Albus said as it picked up the puretree sapling and began digging a small spot in the ground. He buried the plant's roots, making little particles appear around its leaves. This was proof enough that the divine venom in the area was being purified.

"Now all we need to do is watch over the sapling."

"How long will that take?"

"Kousuke claims that the purification will reach around twenty meters in radius within two days. We can call the grand duke here after that."

"Huh?! That's barely anything for two days... Is the plant really gonna be able to affect the whole country?"

"It will work. The speed of purification is set to increase exponentially with the tree's size. Albus, we'll be counting on you to guard it," Bastet said.

"Understood," Albus replied, then nodded in Bastet's direction.

Anubis suddenly turned his head towards the woodland. He growled and continued, "The forest-dwellers are coming."

Three little green-skinned monsters appeared from the underbrush. They were goblins. Territorial little creatures that were instinctively driven to chase out intruders. They wielded clubs and spears and weren't exactly the negotiating type.

Bastet and company looked like a black cat, a black dog, and a little armored person. If the goblins didn't stink so badly themselves, they'd have noticed that the creatures in their path had no discernible scents.

"Gyehgyeeeeh!" "Gyiiih!" "Gyeeegh!"

The three goblins charged forward, probably thinking they had found their meals for the day. But they hadn't found easy targets. Far from it, in fact.

Anubis caught one of them by the throat, seizing it in his jaws and slamming it into the ground. The dog's phrasium fangs sliced through the goblin's flesh like soft butter, ending its life. Meanwhile, Albus' crystal blade severed the heads of the other two. The battle was over before it had even really begun.

"Good work, Albus. Thank you."

"Not a problem," Albus replied and sheathed its blade after nodding at Bastet.

"Sis, Sis! Praise me too!"

"Wooow. You're so great and amazing and impressive."

"Wh-Why so monotone?! I wanted you to mean it!" Anubis began rolling around on the ground and wailing in complaint.

"Don't mess around. Pay attention to our surroundings. If it's just monsters like those goblins that's fine... But if we fail to notice mutants closing in, we'll be done for."

"Pssh..."

Albus could handle a small handful of mutants, but they wouldn't be able to fend off a group with sustained reinforcements. Ideally, they'd just kill any mutants that came near before the group got too large. That was the best way to stall for time.

They had to hold out for two days. If they were lucky, they'd be able to nurture the puretree without any mutants showing up. If they managed that, then they'd be able to leave things to the grand duke and his family.

Bastet glanced toward the sapling for a moment before turning her senses to the surrounding environment.

The mace clashed against the raging halberd. The two wielders passed each other, made a U-turn, and immediately clashed again. The two of them clashed with perfect balance, even though their sizes suggested that to be quite a difficult feat.

I was watching two Frame Gears facing off against each other. One was white, one was blue. Both of them were riding atop their own surfboard-like mounts. Lain, Commander of Brunhild's knight order, was in her Shining Count. Clashing against her was one of her direct subordinates. It was Norn, in her Blue Moon. No, wait, Norn didn't go by Norn anymore. She had changed her name to Nore.

The beastwoman vice-commander came up to me and said it was too confusing having two Norns around in Brunhild, so she took the initiative and changed her name. Apparently, it was less of changing her name, and more of making it sound like the root word of the name, which was pronounced something like Noruen.

Either way, there was now no more confusion. We had Norn, the master of the black crown, and we had Nore, the beastwoman vice-commander of our knights. Apparently, the two of them got along quite well, which might have been because they shared the same name.

Norn looked like a little girl, but was quite the cool-headed individual. Nore, on the other hand, looked older, but was still somewhat child-like in many aspects. The two of them were just about polar opposites in every imaginable way.

As I thought about that, the white and blue knights came to a halt and began attacking each other.

"Hmm, I see... They're not able to use the ground for support, so they're relegated to only attacking with the upper body."

"Yeah. They can't jump around or use any fancy footwork, so this definitely wouldn't work well with Elze's Gerhilde," I casually responded to Nikola, our other vice-commander, who was standing by my side.

Doc Babylon initially thought of fusing Gerhilde with Helmwige, but the idea was scrapped pretty quickly. The flight units that we'd used in the fight against the witch-king were tweaked and given extended durations, then they were passed on to Yae and Hilde's Frame Gears. These flight gears, the floating discs, were only set to be used alongside Knight Barons and Chevaliers.

They weren't really suited to the Frame Gears used by Yumina and the others.

"Most of the flying mutants are the type to charge and attack instead of holding still, so it's a matter of figuring out their timing and making your own lunging strike count."

The flying mutants moved like birds in flight or fish swimming without a current. Most of them launched themselves forward like bullets, taking advantage of their study forms. Though, there were also slower ones that fired crystal fragments, like artillery systems. That was why the best way to win an airborne battle was to determine which types were which, then attack them based on that intel.

"It'll be a bit rough to deal with the ones on the ground using the flight gears."

"Yeah. If they swoop down too low, they'll just get in the way of their allies. It might be a bit hard for them to switch to their shields for a ground-based fight in the midst of all that... Oh dear."

Oh dear... Oh...deer... Nikola's comment reminded me of the other thing that was nearby. I turned around and glanced at the massive mechanical deer that was scampering around. It was our newest Over Gear, Deer Blau. The thing was just a bit larger than our regular Frame Gears.

Over Gears could only be piloted by crown Gollems, which meant that Distortion Blau was currently inside that thing. But that also meant...

"Ooh! Stupendous! Utterly superb! It's moving in accordance with my very will! Brilliant!"

Prince Robert was here... And his voice was blaring out of the speakers. The only person who responded to his joyful yelling was Ceres, his fiancee. She was clapping and cheering for him, a broad smile on her face. The two of them were certainly close...

Norn's Leo Noir and Nia's Tiger Rouge were offense-oriented Over Gears. On the other hand, Robert's Deer Blau was designed with defense in mind. The enormous horns jutting from its forehead were able to deploy magical barriers that it could use to guard the nearby area. That didn't mean it had no offensive capabilities, though. Those horns could also be used to charge the enemy.

Doc Babylon spent a long time deliberating whether to build a horse or a deer, but ultimately she settled on the deer. I didn't exactly have high hopes for the three crown holders working in perfect tandem, but I was appreciative of the increase in raw power we had gained. Though, to be honest, the fact that all three of them were equally likely to let loose and rampage a bit made me worried.

"Not bad, huh? Deer Blau was built especially to make use of that blue crown's ability," Doc Babylon said as she walked up from behind us with Rosetta in tow. She had an ether cigarette in her mouth. At a glance, you'd think it was tobacco, but apparently, it was a special herb that produced a soothing scent. Personally, I thought there was more to it, not to mention the fact that the image of a little girl smoking something like that looked a bit sketchy to those not in the know...

"Is that safe, actually? I kind of think Blau's skill is a bit dangerous..."

"On the contrary! Blau's skill is the one with the least risky price to pay. Nia could bleed out in exchange for power, and Norn could turn into a teeny little embryo and splat on the floor. But that prince? Why, he just takes a nap."

"Sure, but what if he uses too much power and takes a permanent one?"

It wasn't exactly the same as dying, but functionally it was pretty close. I wouldn't want to spend the rest of my life unconscious.

"Don't worry about it. I know I said we're using Blau's ability but we're really only using a fragment of that power. Not nearly enough to be able to kill the prince, either. Plus, I'm sure we could whip something up to wake him in a worst-case scenario... Why, I actually haven't slept in four days, myself." Doctor Babylon let out a strange little laugh after saying that. I felt a bit bad, since we'd clearly been putting a lot of pressure on the R&D staff lately.

Doc Babylon had a gynoid body like the Babylon numbers, which meant she could keep on operating without sleep for far longer than a human being... Still, her brain was that of a human's, so she needed her rest every now and then.

"You should go and sleep, Doc. You don't want to put your health or life at risk, do you?"

The Guinness Book of World Records actually stopped taking participants who were going for the record of the longest time without sleep. They were worried someone would kill themselves during an attempt.

"I can't sleep until I see my projects through, Touya. But I wouldn't mind a reward from you... I've been working extra hard lately, after all."

"...A reward? Like what?"

I looked down at the doc, who was staring up at me with bags under her eyes. So long as her request wasn't too difficult, I was happy to give her something for all the hard work she'd been doing.

"Nothing too bad, really. I was thinking a steamy night, you and I...my legs locked around your waist, and..."

"Oh, I see. You want me to knock you out and force you to go to sleep, huh?"

Her idea was definitely not happening. I should have expected no less from a dirty little deviant like her, but I'd hoped for something better. It was honestly frightening just how straight-faced she said it, looking up at me with those tired eyes.

"Then I want you to hold me. I want a hug, Touya… Just a hug."

She'd certainly lowered the bar. I wondered if she was using that negotiating tactic where you highball an offer hoping for an intentional failure, then pretend to negotiate down toward what you actually wanted. I was pretty sure that was known as the door-in-the-face method. Doc Babylon held her arms out, so I complied with her request and lifted her up.

"Hehehehe… It's been a while since I've been this close to your body, Touya… I like it. It's getting me in the mood…"

"…I can still wrestle you off me."

Doc Babylon wrapped her legs around my waist and held on to my body with her arms, using all the strength in her body. She was basically like a koala clinging to a eucalyptus tree! It wasn't a hug anymore, it was just her holding on tight.

Suddenly, I felt the strength drain from her limbs and soft breaths waft from her lips. I moved my arms to support her. *Huh? Wait a sec…*

"She's asleep! Yessir, she is!"

"Geez…" I heaved a sigh as Rosetta spoke. She was looking over Doc Babylon from the side. I definitely couldn't set her down at this point… Part of me wondered if she was just pretending, honestly.

"...She really did work hard, yessir. She really did..."

"Hm?"

"Five thousand years back...she was a genius of the time, yessir, she was. She only ever worked on what she wanted to work on. She did all her experiments without thinking about anyone else."

"Isn't that basically the same as now...?"

"Sir, no, sir! She never once used her genius for anyone else's sake. Never... If you want my opinion, sir, she crossed five thousand years in that suspended animation just so she could meet you. So she could be here for you."

...That would take some pretty intense feelings... It's true that she's been an invaluable asset, though...

"All of us Babylon gynoids care deeply for you, sir. But that isn't just because you're the heir of Babylon. It isn't just because you're the owner of the floating fortress, no, sir. It's because our personalities all stem from her, sir," Rosetta said as she pointed at the sleeping doctor, giving a small smile. I'd never thought about it like that before. She wasn't wrong, though. Hell, the Babylon islands had been designed so I was the only one who could take control of them. Even though I had to fulfill certain conditions to master each individual piece, the whole thing had been planned with me in mind. It was a pretty impressive deception.

Doctor Babylon had peeked into the future. She knew I was the only person in this era with every elemental aptitude. She'd set the events in motion that resulted in me acquiring Babylon. Everything had proceeded according to her plan... Which was fine, in the end, since it had saved us.

"She's a little heavy here... Rosetta, can you carry her on your back?"

"Sir, yes, sir!" Rosetta turned around and crouched as she said that, so I placed the sleeping doctor on her back.

"Have her sleep a while in the ramparts. And, uh...when she wakes up, could you thank her for me?"

"Oh, sir? Did you finally warm up to her?"

"Shut up!"

Rosetta smiled and walked forward, then beamed up to Babylon. She'd done a lot for us, so there was no way our paths could untwine at this point. But honestly...I didn't want to lose her. She'd become important to me.

Just a few days later, we would march upon Isengard and start the final conflict against the wicked god. I vowed to drag out the enemy and put an end to all this strife. Though, in all honesty, I was worried more about the stuff that would come afterward. I had my wedding to fret about, as well as my divine training...

But still, I had to face it head-on.

"Auugh! Why did this have to happen?!" Bastet let out a small sigh as she watched the mutant dissolve in front of her.

"Mm. We were discovered too soon," Albus stated as he sheathed his crystal blade and glanced around the area.

"Why was there a mutant here, huh?! It makes no sense!"

It was a terrible stroke of bad luck. Bastet, Anubis, and Albus had been discovered far earlier than they should have been. It hadn't even been a day. The death of the lone variant that had found them would surely herald the arrival of more.

"Should we run back to Brunhild? We can use that magic mirror!"

"And abandon the puretree? No way. It's growing quite nicely," Bastet said, nodding toward the tree, which was already over a meter tall. If they returned to Brunhild, the three of them would be safe from harm, but...the puretree would be completely defenseless, and they'd have to start everything from scratch.

A large-scale attack from the mutants wasn't guaranteed. Even if they did show up, it wouldn't be that big of a group. They'd be able to handle it... Or so Bastet hoped, at least. Ideally, no enemies would show up, though.

"Thirty meters ahead. Five enemies. Mutants," Albus spoke as he unsheathed his blade again. Bastet groaned, her prayers unanswered, but she positioned herself in front of the puretree to defend it. Albus and Anubis stood before Bastet. There were less of them than there were mutants, so the fight would be a tough one.

Albus was a crown, the apex of Gollem technology, but Yumina wasn't around to issue proper commands. In its current state, Albus would be operating at around ten percent of its full power. A Gollem could only reveal its true strength when fighting in tandem with its master. This rule applied for Bastet and Anubis too. However, despite all that, they had no choice but to fight the enemy.

"Victory goes to those who act first," Albus proclaimed as he dashed ahead at the mutants who appeared.

A crawfish-shaped mutant raised its pincers and aimed them at the Gollems. A few spheres of light gathered within the open pincers, and they began shooting out laser beams. Albus dodged them, slicing one of the pincers off neatly. The Gollem then swerved to the side and plunged its blade into the mutant's side.

Unfortunately, the mutant didn't stop moving. Instead, it merely swung its other pincer at Albus. Albus responded by slicing off that pincer as well, then drove its blade through the enemy's head.

The mutant finally stopped moving, and it began to melt into a puddle of goo. Albus' final strike had located the core and sliced it in two. Unlike the regular Phrase, mutants didn't have visible cores, so it was a case of guesswork to find out how to finish them off for good.

"Albus! Get these guys as well!" Anubis called out for help as he frantically dodged the two mutants by his side.

Anubis and Bastet didn't just have [Storage] available to them, but also [Accel], [Shield], [Fly], and [Invisible]. They were all defensive or utility-oriented skills, but [Invisible] was basically useless against the mutants to begin with. They didn't even have eyes.

They did have [Paralyze] and [Gravity] on their forelegs, but paralysis was ineffective on the mutants. Plus, the gravity-manipulation only increased the force of their crystal claws, so it wouldn't do too much against them, either.

Albus tried to kill the mutants harassing Anubis, but it wasn't going so well. And Bastet was also having trouble defending the puretree more directly.

The mutants were currently attacking the three Gollems. If they all fled from the area, there was a good chance the enemy would give chase and ignore the puretree... But that was a gamble that Bastet didn't want to take.

"Ack, things are getting rough!"

Another crayfish mutant swept in to attack Bastet, making her panic. And right when she decided that retreating would probably be a good idea, she heard a strange voice call out.

"Oh me, oh my... A cute little puppy and a sweet little kitty? How quaint and curious! We should get in on this too, hehehe!"

"Wh—?!"

A girl had appeared as if from nowhere. She looked quite out of place. She was wearing a pretty purple dress. Her eyes were amethyst, matching the color of her hair, and she wielded a small parasol that leaned against her shoulder.

But the thing that shocked Bastet the most wasn't the girl. It was the tiny purple Gollem by her side. The one wielding a scythe twice its own size.

The machine looked startlingly similar to Albus...

"A...wicked god?"

"Yes. Well, we're calling it that, but it's not really a god... Just think of it as the top dog of the mutants. In other words, their leader."

We were within one of Brunhild's conference rooms. I was currently hosting a meeting with all of the world leaders in hopes of addressing the Isengard situation. I told them that the mutants had made a home in Isengard and that their leader was on the verge of awakening. I also told them that the mutants were running wild, and that the landmass had a special kind of curse on it that we were close to dispelling.

"And what will happen when this wicked god wakes up?" the beastking leaned forward as he spoke.

"I can't say for sure, but...I think the mutants will be spread across the whole world. They feed on souls, and those that have their souls eaten by it will transform into skeletal mutants and bolster the enemy ranks. It's likely that their aim is to transform all humans, or all living creatures in the world, into mutants."

Everyone believed me at face value. After all, we'd all fought against the mutants, or at least seen videos of them in action.

"I don't plan to take that lying down, though. Right now, a special kind of venom is blocking the way to the wicked god, but we've planted a special tree that can purify it. Once the purification reaches their main base of operations, we'll move in and take out the enemy leader."

"Are you certain you can handle that?" the queen of Strain raised her hand as she asked that question, and I nodded in response.

"We can, yes. I promise you that. I have a wedding to deal with after this, so I can't afford to die there. We head on over and take it out."

"Ahahaha! Sounds like a hell of a reason, champ!" the king of Felsen laughed uproariously in response to my statement, his muscles rippling as he shook. His over-the-top response made the other world leaders smile in turn.

"So then, what do we do?"

"Once they realize the puretree can dispel their curse, the wicked god will likely charge toward it. That's when I'll head toward the wicked god. While I'm doing that, I want the alliance to use the Frame Gears to defend the tree."

I didn't think they had a particularly large army of mutants left, but I couldn't exactly be sure... There were definitely a hell of a lot of those golden Skeletons, but they wouldn't be able to put up a fight against our Frame Gears.

"Interesting... So by protecting the puretree, we protect the world..." the emperor of Regulus muttered and stroked his beard.

"Indeed. A rather simple solution. I would be glad to join hands with you all in defense of our world. This wicked god cannot do as it pleases with our newly unified alliance!"

The king of Belfast's words rippled through the air, making everyone nod in agreement.

It was obvious we'd all have to band together if the world was at stake. It was in our best interests to survive. No creature was going to just sit there and let itself die. But the same could be said of our enemies. It was kill or be killed. A simple situation. Our opponents couldn't be negotiated with, so they had to die.

"It's hard to say what they'll do if we back them into a corner. We have a lot of measures in place, but it's possible we can't communicate properly when we're in enemy territory. That's why we thought up this plan..." I told everyone about my secret emergency strategy. Ideally, we wouldn't have to employ it, but it was best to be prepared. I didn't want to fail because we hadn't considered every option.

Once the meeting ended, we all headed toward the afterparty. Everyone relaxed and began to enjoy the celebration, hoping that it wouldn't be the last.

"I think things'll be fine now that we've learned about your secret strategy, Touya. I'm quite amazed you even thought something like that up."

"Yeah... I'd prefer it if we didn't have to resort to that, though."

"Oh, aye? I'm quite eager to give it a shot! Sounds like it'll be a riot!"

The beastking grinned broadly as he spoke. I wasn't surprised. Just like the ruler of Lassei, he loved nothing more than a good fight.

The beastking laughed a bit more before heading off to the training grounds. He was going to have a sparring match with the Lassei potentate. I felt a little bit sorry for his retainers, who walked after him while letting out quiet sighs.

"G-Grand Duke!" I turned to see the Ramissh pope charging toward me at full pelt. To be honest, I was worried about her running so quickly, given her age... I had more than enough tact to keep that thought internal, though.

"I-I was speaking with your head maid, and she informed me that your grandfather is here?! C-Could I speak with him, perhaps?"

Hey, hey... Back up a little! You're getting a bit close to me... Even your paladins are getting all confused, ma'am... I wasn't too surprised to see her freaking out this way, given she was basically the world's most devoted fan of God Almighty, but it was still a bit much.

"Uhhh... He's having tea with Karen and the others right now, I think."

"Wh-Where?!"

"Should be in the castle lounge?"

"I'll be off, then! Thank you!" Her Holiness charged away, leaving her hapless paladins to run after her.

I was honestly a little bit freaked out by the encounter. Still, the old man seemed to enjoy talking with the pope, so I had a feeling it'd all work out.

"Was that the pope of Ramissh? What just happened?"

The holy king of Allent walked up to me, glass of wine in hand, as he asked me that question.

"Oh, I wouldn't worry about it. Just one of those things." His country was religious too, so I didn't really want him finding out about God Almighty.

The Allent Theocracy was a nation of devout spirit worshipers. They considered spirits to be messengers from the divine, so they prayed to them. Apparently, the current leader of Allent was extra-popular with his people because we helped him communicate with the spirits directly. His popularity made sense, given that he'd done something no leader had managed in the past.

"Have you managed to confer with a spirit on your own yet?"

"No, not yet. It would seem my magical reserves don't run too deeply. Speaking in the tongue of the spirits is also proving somewhat difficult."

"You do have some magical aptitude, though?"

"Indeed, I do. I checked with one of those small spellstones. I appear to be suited to the wind element, though I've yet to perform even an elementary Wind spell."

Wind, huh…? Most of the lesser Wind Spirits are pretty curious by nature, so they should be responding… Having the aptitude for an element makes you more likely to have an affinity with the spirits of that element. It's probably the fact that he's not good at speaking their language.

"Could you speak a bit of that spirit tongue for me?"

"Right here?"

The man blushed in slight embarrassment as he recited the spirit-summoning verse. I immediately understood what the issue was…

"It's your pronunciation that's the issue. You're not saying the word 'gale' properly."

"Huh? Gale?"

"Yeah… You were saying the incantation wrong. Just now, you said, well… You said, 'Please heed my call, O spirit of the… whale.'"

"Wh-Whale?!" the king before me exclaimed, blank-faced and shocked. His soldiers behind him desperately tried to hold in their laughter.

Well, these things happen… You try to summon a specific spirit, but accidentally call out the wrong one… In cases like that, the spirit will realize it wasn't meant to be summoned and vanish without a trace. The whimsical Wind Spirits would definitely just flitter away too. They'd leave the moment they learned they weren't actually invited.

There was no such thing as a whale spirit, either. There were definitely Water Spirits, but nothing like that...

We spent about ten minutes teaching him the differences between the words "whale" and "gale" in spirit tongue until he finally got the pronunciation down. Well, it still came out a little weird. He said it more like "gwale," but it was at least close enough.

We were indoors, but being near an open window was good enough for a Wind Spirit. I told him to stand by the window and try the incantation properly. Once he did, a little spirit appeared before him. It was a small girl who could fit into his palm.

"I-It worked!"

I pushed him to forge a contract with the spirit. His words sounded a bit wonky, but the meaning was conveyed properly.

The lesser spirit rose into the air and swirled around him before perching on his hand and vanishing in a flash. However, a tiny stone remained in his hand where the spirit had been.

"Good job, you forged the contract properly."

"Amazing! I really did it! Oh my! A blessed spirit has come to me at last!"

"To call the spirit back, hold the stone and draw on the feelings from within. Don't issue orders to it or anything, just treat it as if it was a friend."

"V-Very well!"

I didn't want to put a damper on his happiness, but it was better to call the spirit back when the feelings were still fresh. That way, it would be easier to call them in the future. Plus, it would've been bad if the spirit was contracted and then never called out after a while, like a guy confessing his feelings to a girl, then never actually scheduling a date until a month later. So I guess in a sense, this situation would be like going on a date right after the confession...

As my mind wandered, the spirit appeared again and began dancing through the air.

"Ohhh! She came! She's here!"

The king jumped for joy. I was a bit relieved to see it, since it clearly meant the environment of his nation was well-maintained.

Spirits didn't have a habit of sticking around in nations that treated them poorly. If I remembered right, there were no spirits in Isengard anymore... That meant the land would lose its fertility, the water would become muddied and filthy, and the winds would only blow stagnant air.

I didn't think people would be able to survive in a wasteland like that. And that was why it was more important than ever for us to fulfill our mission. I hoped that the three Gollems in Isengard were looking after the puretree properly. After all, I had no means of knowing if Bastet and the others were okay.

"Huuuh? You're not a real kitty and puppy? That's so sad! I wanted to pry out your little eyeballs and feel them squelch into mush under my fingers... That's such a shame, geez..."

Bastet cowered in fear at the girl before her. The purple beauty spoke casually, but the subject matter of her speech was exceptionally vile. As she spoke, the purple Gollem finished slicing up the last mutant to pieces.

Its body was far too close to Albus, the white crown. This purple Gollem was clearly another of the crown series.

Bastet's memories from her time in the Death Wings bandit gang were still there. During that time, she had learned of the crowns that existed in the world. There was the Panaches Kingdom's Distortion Blau, the blue one. There was the Red Cat's Blood Rouge, the red one. Then, there was also the Rhea Kingdom of Elves' Grand Grun, the green one.

But there was one other crown that was known across the lands. It was the purple crown, Fanatic Viola, contracted partner of Luna Trieste, the Frenzied Mistress. It was a death herald that spread chaos and misery in its wake. And at the moment, that Gollem was standing right in front of Bastet.

"Hey, who does that little white cutie belong to? It's a crown like my Viola! It's our first time meeting, honey! Can I get your name?"

"I am Albus. My master is not in the vicinity."

"Oh my... You're all alone? Who's your master?"

"My Master is Yumina Ernea Belfast, queen of the Duchy of Brunhild, wife to Mochizuki Touya."

Yumina wasn't actually the queen yet, but Albus' databanks didn't seem to care. Luna actually seemed startled by the Gollem's words, blinking a few times in surprise.

"Mochizuki...Touya?! Whaaat?! No way! No way! Little Tou's a world leader! Tell me more, I need to know more!" Luna scooted closer to Albus with amazed eyes as she shrieked those words. Albus wasn't in the least bit concerned about the sudden motion, but the animal Gollems were suspicious.

"Hey, lady. What's your relationship with our grand duke?" Anubis raised the question, secretly hoping that this mysterious woman was a newfound ally.

"Mm... Me and Tou? We're like lovers, I guess! I try to murder him, then he tries to murder me... It's really lovey-dovey and erotic."

"Uh... Okay..."

The Gollem grimaced slightly, which was impressive given his lack of a human face. After that, he started to back off.

"So...Tou isn't here, huh? That's so sad! I wanted us to mutilate each other..."

"...He will be picking us up from this location tomorrow. In the meantime, we're defending the area."

"Defending?" Luna raised a brow in response to Bastet's statement. Then, a golden spear flew in from out of nowhere and pierced through Luna's belly. It wasn't actually a spear, though. It was the sharpened limb of a mutant that had appeared in the area.

It had the form of a Japanese spider crab and had extended its limb to stab Luna from over twenty meters away. Blood began to spurt from the open wound, but then it suddenly stopped. Luna twisted her body, breaking off the embedded limb at her back.

"You dummy! I'm trying to have a conversation here!" Luna roared, swinging her right arm back. It quickly morphed into a long, golden blade that bisected the mutant and multiple nearby trees.

Bastet and Anubis were utterly horrified. The power she had just displayed was unmistakably that of the mutants they were facing. They couldn't get a feel for the situation, but felt it safe to assume she wasn't working with the mutants. That didn't necessarily mean she was their friend, though.

"Beep..." Viola charged ahead into the forest. It mowed down several crab-like mutants that had come out from the treeline. The mutants tried to counter, but the brutal attacks they unleashed on the little Gollem did nothing to deter it. It didn't even bother trying to dodge. Why would it, when it could regenerate from all the damage?

The power of the purple crown was unmatched regeneration ability. It was a monstrous power that ate away at the mind of the Gollem's master as compensation. Luna's belly, once sliced open, had completely resealed itself. The torn clothing around the wound, however, stayed the same.

Bastet could only feel intense dread when faced with this duo. However, her Q-Crystal mind was telling her that they could make use of these frightening strangers. Most Gollems had emotions, but they were still machines at the base. It was only natural for them to prioritize the pragmatic option.

"...Lady Luna, would you like to meet our grand duke, Touya?"

"I really would, yes! Tou's such a shy little boy, so he always runs away... Is he coming here, little kitty? Or am I wasting my time?"

"I'm set to bring him here tomorrow. You can meet him if you stay here."

"No waaay! I wanna see him right now! Can't you call him over, little kitty? Or maybe you can show me to him?"

"I'm afraid I cannot, my lady. If I go home before the ordained time, then they will believe the mission has failed. Sir Touya will have no reason to come here. Plus, the method of transportation can only be used by Gollems, so I can't take you with me," Bastet steeled her mind before letting out those words. Unfortunately, they seemed to greatly displease Luna.

"Boo..."

Half of that statement was a lie. The mirror they had would definitely let a human pass through, but Bastet was prepared to use any means necessary to get Luna to stay.

"Tsk... Well, okay! I'll just have to meet him when he comes here tomorrow. Oh, my clothes are such a mess! I'll need to change before Tou comes and sees me. I look so indecent!"

Luna produced a storage card from her skirt and tapped on it, making a fresh change of clothes appeared on the ground in front of her. Then, she immediately stripped off her outfit and began changing into the new one.

Bastet let out a small sigh of relief. Or, well, not exactly, since Gollems didn't actually breathe, but she felt it appropriate to make the gesture.

"Is this okay, Sis? They might fight as soon as he arrives..." Anubis walked over to Bastet and whispered softly.

"That isn't our problem. Our mission is to defend the puretree, right? I'm sure our grand duke will be able to handle her. He didn't reach gold rank status for no reason."

Luna and Viola were a fearsome duo, and their regeneration effectively made them impervious to harm. Despite all that, Bastet firmly believed the grand duke of Brunhild was more than a match for them.

All they had to do was hold out for one more day. So long as they could manage that, the grand duke and his companions would take care of the rest. Bastet held that determination close to her heart as she anxiously glanced back at the puretree.

"Hey, pal. Sorry about calling you out here."

"It's all good. What's the issue?"

Ende had called me over on the phone, so I'd headed over to his house. The three Phrase girls were there as well. I hadn't actually been inside their home before, so the first thing I noticed was that it was a bit drab and simplistic. There weren't even any vases with flowers in them.

The three Dominant Constructs in the house were hungry as ever. They'd been chowing down on a huge pile of dango and daifuku mochi. They weren't eating them especially fast, but they were picking up more food even as they sipped their tea...

I didn't want to know their food budget. It probably rivaled our national budget...

"I want to talk about Yula's side," Melle, who had finished sipping her tea, set down her cup on the table as she said that.

...I can't really take that dire expression seriously when there's sauce on your cheeks...

"We can sense the presence of the mutants who were formerly our kin. Most of them are gathered in Isengard right now, but we sensed a special aura amongst them."

"Huh? Do you mean the wicked god?"

Ende and the girls knew about the god situation, and they knew about the wicked god as well. My searching skill couldn't detect the wicked god because of the divine venom, but I wondered if they could.

"No, it's not the wicked god. We're unable to sense that creature. We sensed a new Dominant Construct... Well, it's more accurate to say it's a Dominant Construct we remember."

Huh? Is that the creature I saw through the crack in reality earlier? It must have come through to Isengard during the emergence event... But what does she mean by one she remembers?

"Yula likely summoned him from Phrasia. The aura he emits is unmistakable... It's the presence of Xeno, the Phrase general."

"Huh...? There's a Phrase general?"

"Phrasia, our home planet, is a desolate place. There are monsters similar to magical beasts, and several invasive species that compete for dominion. We classify Dominant Constructs differently, and there's a special classification for those that have survived many battles. I'll refer to them as the combat strain... Anyway, the apex of this strain is General Xeno. Lycee and I are Lady Melle's advisors, so putting us aside, you can consider Yula to be the apex of the civil strain,"

Ney spoke, spraying little crumbs of dango out of her mouth all the while.

"Is he powerful?"

"Immensely. He's Gila's elder brother. He definitely isn't as coarse as Gila was, but he lives for battle."

Gila... So he was part of the combat strain too, huh? He definitely seemed like the kind of guy who loved to fight, so I guess it makes sense his brother is similar.

"General Xeno... Well, it seems he has brought over many of his subordinate Dominant Constructs with him. I don't recognize any of their auras, so they probably joined up with him after I began crossing through worlds."

"Tsk... It was bad enough when it was just Yula and the wicked god, but now we have to deal with this?"

If it's another hothead like Gila, then I guess I'll have to put off my showdown with the wicked god for now...

"Fret not about that. We'll take down Xeno. You should focus your efforts on the wicked god," Melle said, suddenly dispelling my thoughts. Ney, Lycee, and Ende nodded in agreement.

"Matters concerning the Phrase should be handled by the Phrase. We'll use the upcoming battle to rid the multiverse of these corroded links in our chain. This all began because of what I did with Endymion, so I am responsible for handling the fallout, as the Phrase Sovereign."

Well...I mean, it was technically my fault that the servile god escaped and triggered the birth of the wicked god to begin with... That's also why the mutants exist now too... W-Wait, are you snidely trying to tell me to take responsibility?! Well, whatever. I'm just glad these guys want to help out. That reminds me, I should tell them about my strategy...

"Hm? An emergency plan?"

"Yeah. We don't know how things will actually go down. Yula could pull a dirty trick on us. That's why I thought of this plan..." I explained the secret plan to Ende and the girls.

"Huh? Is that really possible?"

"Temporarily, yes. I've tested it already. If it comes down to it, you'll have to just roll with it."

"If you really can do that, then I'm sure we'll be able to best anything Yula throws our way. But this whole thing feels a little..."

"Absurd..." Ney folded her arms slightly, an uncertain expression on her face, as Lycee finished her sentence. Personally, I thought calling my plan absurd was a little mean. But still, I simply shrugged and lent the two sacred treasure blades to Ney and Lycee. I didn't want to run the risk of them being contaminated by the mutants.

"This is for you, Ende."

"Oh? You have something for me?"

I pulled a pair of gauntlets out from my [Storage]. They were made from dense phrasium. I only realized in hindsight that it was a bit insensitive to bring out a weapon like that in front of the Phrase girls.

"They're the same as the ones Elze uses. You'll be able to take out the mutants easier like that."

"I don't exactly use weapons when I fight, but I'm sure they'll come in handy..." Ende said as he took the pellucid gauntlets from me. The material was the same as Elze's, but the design was different. That was completely intentional on my part, since I didn't want it looking like he was paired up with my fiancee.

"Oh, right. Will my master be joining us against the wicked god?"

"He won't. We'll be doing this all by ourselves, with no guidance from them. They'll help us defend the puretree, but nothing more than that. That being said, they'll be keeping an eye on the battle... so you should probably do your best. If you screw up or don't fight all that well, Uncle Takeru'll probably put you through hell afterward."

"D-Don't say things like that, man!" Ende cried out, small tears welling up in his eyes. I felt sorry for him, but that wasn't really my problem. I needed to make sure Ende was motivated to fight as hard as he could. The revelation of Xeno's involvement was just too troubling this late in the game. I couldn't have my plans dashed when everything was going so well.

Bastet would be reporting back in a day. After that, it would be off to Isengard.

I wanted to send Moroha and Karina in first, but I felt that sending people with high levels of divinity into an area with poison surrounding it was a bad idea. We'd have to wait a bit longer for the purification to reach a wider radius.

I could've gone too, but I didn't want any negative side effects caused by the venom. If I fell before the decisive battle, it'd basically be a sick joke.

That was why we were sending in people who wouldn't be as affected first. That meant Norn, Nia, and Robert. The crowns would be our safest bet. Even without their Over Gears, they'd be able to fight pretty well. If they were pushed into a defensive battle, they'd only have to hold out a bit before the rest of us got there.

I left Ende's house, called up Robert, and asked for his help. I could hear his pumpkin pants rustling. He was a really weird guy, but he was also clearly a sincere and earnest person. If he could just get rid of the freaky fashion sense and the strange attitude, he'd have been a model prince...

In Norn's case, I decided to just ask Elluka to speak to her on my behalf. Given that we'd granted refuge and work to Elluka, I couldn't imagine the girl rejecting us.

The main issue was probably Nia. The Red Cats weren't exactly doing any chivalrous thievery at the moment, since I hadn't permitted any crimes in Brunhild. Chivalrous or not, thievery was still thievery. And because of that, they'd basically turned to adventuring. They'd done a lot of dungeon diving and came back with a fair share of treasure.

It was honestly more apt to call them an adventuring party at this point. They had Nia's red crown, and Est's Akagane helping them out, so they were doing quite nicely.

"If it was just Nia, then I could probably get her to come along… But Est's too shrewd. There's no way she'll make the Red Cats help out for free."

I sighed quietly, hoping we could work out a good deal. Then, I headed to the Silver Moon to negotiate with the Red Cats, although really, the negotiation would just be with Est.

The sky had brightened.

They were within a dense forest, so it wasn't like they could see the sun, but it was still clear that morning had come.

The mutants, who had decreed them to be enemies in their territory, had not stopped attacking all night. But they didn't attack in a large group. Instead, they kept on coming in waves of five to six at a time. Even Bastet, a Gollem that had no need for sleep, was beginning to feel weary.

But there was one human…if you could even call her that… who had faced the mutants non-stop without so much as a hint of exhaustion.

"Kitty, kitty! It's morning time! Are you gonna call little Tou over? I'm ready!" Luna giggled with glee as she shattered an enemy's core. Interestingly enough, she was able to precisely pinpoint where a mutant's weak spots were. It was possible she gained this ability after gaining the mutant's power herself.

"Sis… It might be a little early, but we do need to tell the grand duke about this lady, so…"

"Indeed…" Bastet looked over to the white Gollem by her side. Albus nodded in response.

The puretree behind Bastet was now four meters tall. Luna and her purple crown had reduced all the other trees in the area to stumps with their wild slashing. Anubis had dutifully picked up all the fallen trees with his [Storage] collar, then dumped them elsewhere.

Anubis was right in that it was a little early to head back and report in, but they were dealing with some unusual circumstances. It probably wouldn't have been such a bad idea to report a little sooner than expected.

"Very well, then. It may take a little time, but I'll report to the grand duke."

"Ohhh, perfect! Aaah, mmh… I really can't wait! I want to be with my little Tou… We'll thrust into each other, we'll asphyxiate each other…crush each other… It'll be just perfect!"

Bastet and Anubis backed up a little, clearly disturbed by the woman's muttering.

"Anubis."

"Aye aye!" Anubis used his [**Storage**] collar to eject the full one-and-a-half-meter tall mirror.

Albus then picked it up and propped it by a nearby tree stump.

"Very well. I'll return with the grand duke in about an hour."

"Hurry, hurry. Don't be too long, kitty!" Luna said as she smiled and waved, but that just made Bastet feel worse. She turned toward Anubis, giving a glance that tried to say, "I'll leave the rest to you." However, her glance was registered as an aggressive stare by the dog Gollem, who had no idea what he'd done wrong.

Bastet sighed and hopped through the mirror portal.

The mirror was connected to a room in Brunhild castle known as the mirror hall. There were various mirrors in the room, connected to places like Drakliff island, Brunhild's Belfast embassy, and so on. The room was primarily used by maids and knights that worked in the castle from long distances. Special individuals like Sue had personal mirrors that connected directly to their own bedrooms, so they didn't need to use the hall.

《Hmm? What's a cat doooing here? Oh, are you perhaps the Gooollem that my master spoke of?》

Bastet looked up toward the source of the voice. It had come from a painting that stood at the top of a flight of stairs. It was a painting of a young girl. She had pink, braided hair, and wore a white dress. Though, the most surprising thing about the girl in the painting was that she was leaning halfway out of the frame.

《Nice to meet youuu. I'm Ripple. I wooork as the castle's surveillance system.》

"I see... So you're the artifact creature. I am Bastet. I am a Gollem in the service of Mistress Elluka, who lives in this Duchy at present. Could you contact the grand duke at once? It's an emergency situation."

《Hm? Of cooourse. I'll just—》

"Ohhh. So this is Tou's home? He really does have an eye for pretty things, huh?"

"Wha—?!" Bastet felt a chill run down her spine, which wasn't actually possible because she was a Gollem. She turned around and found, to her horror, that Luna was standing in the hall of mirrors.

"Why are you here?!"

"I wanted to see Tou, so I followed you!" Luna said that, then smiled and winked as a tiny purple Gollem passed through a mirror behind her. It brandished its scythe, which made Bastet grit her mechanical teeth. She had screwed up.

"Intruders in the castle! Notify everyone immediately!"

《Awawawaaah! O-Okaaay!》 Ripple screamed as she shot back into the painting. Since she was a magical lifeform, she had duplicates of her own body in paintings all over the castle. They served as her eyes and ears, allowing her to act as a live surveillance network for the entire area. She could project those copies of herself out of the frame and notify people to sound the alarm.

Ripple sent her copies all over the castle, while her main body went straight to her master's bedroom.

《Maaaster! Maaaster! Wake up! It's an emergency situaaation!》

"Mnh… Five more minutes…"

I woke up to someone bothering me. Then, I rubbed my eyes and rose from the bed before noticing it was Ripple.

"What's up…?"

《Intruders in the caaastle! A tiny purple Gollem with a scythe, and a girl with glaaaaaasses! They're in the mirror haaall!》

I knew exactly what Ripple was describing, and it made me break out into a cold sweat.

A tiny purple Gollem with a scythe… I only knew one Gollem like that.

"It can't be!"

I leaped up and grabbed my smartphone from the side counter, then immediately warped myself to the mirror hall. I hadn't even gotten changed out of my pajamas.

I couldn't see any invaders. Only Bastet was around. She was curled up in a ball near a wall. I could see a small impact dent in the wall above her…which made me immediately guess that Luna had done this to her.

"Hey, are you okay?!"

"G-Grand Duke… I'll be fine… I was blasted back… One of my feet is no longer operating properly… Y-You must stop them, please! Go after Luna Trieste!"

"Damn, so it really is her!"

I clenched my teeth in a panic. I had no idea why such a rotten person had shown up at a crucial moment. I picked up Bastet in my arms and teleported to Babylon's research laboratory. There was nobody around, save for a wolf Gollem who seemed to be resting by a repair platform.

"Touya? And…Bastet?! What happened?!" Fenrir looked up at us in a panic, quickly rising from his sleepy stupor. Fenrir was the Gollem equivalent of a sibling to Bastet and Anubis, so his concern was understandable.

"F-Forgive me, Brother Fenrir… I've failed…"

"Fenrir! Look after Bastet! Get Elluka to check up on her diagnostics!"

I ran off immediately and triggered my searching magic.

"Show me Luna Trieste!"

"…Search complete. Brunhild Castle. Western Corridor, Second Floor. Target is currently engaged in combat."

"Wh-With who?!"

"…Search complete. Mochizuki Moroha and Mochizuki Karina."

When I heard those two names, relief coursed through my body.

My sisters, huh…? Thank goodness. If anyone can deal with her, it's them… Even if she does something crazy… Wait, crap. I can't relax just yet! She could've injured people in the castle!

I used teleport for the third time that morning and warped to where my sisters were. And when I arrived, I found Luna unconscious on the floor, her crown struggling against several arrows that had pinned it to the wall.

Standing over Luna were my two sisters, as well as Yae and Hilde. Apparently, they'd encountered Luna on their way to morning practice.

"Oh, Touya. Morning."

"Morning, Karina…"

Karina turned around and greeted me, so I answered. However, it felt a little weird doing that given the circumstances.

The hallway was completely wrecked, and there were parts beyond repair. The cracks in the ceiling and walls were probably from Luna's blade arm or Viola's scythe. Viola had also been pinned to the wall, so Karina's arrows were probably stuck pretty deep in there too.

"Listen, Touya, I know you're your own man...but please take some advice from your older sister. Don't stick it in crazy. Ever."

"Whoa, hey! Don't say that! Nobody's been sticking anything anywhere!"

Moroha seemed to be under the impression that I'd had an affair with Luna, and she'd come back to find me and commit some kind of crazy murder-suicide.

"...What is going on here, Touya-dono?"

"Touya? What exactly have you been...sticking...?"

"No! Stop! You've got it all wrong! Please don't glare at me like that! I haven't done anything wrong!" I screamed that and flailed my arms in panic as Yae and Hilde approached me.

Ugh, hey... I didn't do anything, so why do I have to...? Ah... Ahhh... I suddenly had a flashback to the scorching desert, the brightness of the sun, and Luna's naked body as it glistened in the heat.

"Well, let's put Touya's affair aside for a moment."

"My what...?!"

"This girl... She has mutant power inside her. Is that the reason for her strange behavior?"

"Isn't she just crazy 'cause Touya pumped and dumped her?"

"Quit saying that!"

I explained exactly who Luna Trieste was, as well as what Viola did to people who contracted with it, and that I had nothing to do with whatever weird stuff Luna might have said.

I hadn't done anything wrong!

"Hm... So it eats one's sanity? What do you want to do with her, Touya?"

Hmm... For someone as dangerous as her, execution or permanent imprisonment would be best...

I looked over at Viola. Part of me wondered if Luna would be freed from her curse if I killed that Gollem.

But...Viola's regeneration abilities were more than a pain all on their own. Even if I sliced it into little bits, it'd regenerate itself. Then Luna's mental state would be sapped as the compensation for that power. It was a vicious cycle I couldn't realistically break.

"Well, let's think about what to do. But maybe we'll leave the bigger decisions for—"

"Beep."

I was about to finish my sentence when Viola freed itself from the arrows holding it back. It quickly scrambled for its scythe and wasted no time swinging at me.

102

Goddammit! I scowled and cast **[Eternal Coffin]** on the little horror.

"Be-Beep!"

Pillars of ice rose from the floor, coming together to encase the Gollem in a block. Just to be sure, I'd charged the spell with divinity as well. I was sure that even a crown couldn't put a scratch on the ice I'd formed. And so, I quickly severed the ice from the floor to move the block around.

"My liege!"

The knights rushed over, Captain Rebecca at the front. They'd probably been called over by Ripple. Rebecca was an adventurer I'd first met back in the desert along with Logan. Logan was captain of the watch, while she was the captain of the royal guard.

"Forgive us, sir!"

"Don't worry. This wasn't your garden-variety situation."

"...Garden variety? I'm afraid I don't know that saying."

"Oh... Sorry. It's an unusual situation. Please haul this Gollem and this girl to our **[Prison]**-enchanted dungeon... No, wait, Luna can probably break through that with her mutant powers... Give me a sec."

I had a feeling **[Paralyze]** wouldn't do anything to her... And even if it did, I didn't want her constantly soiling herself, either.

As I pondered what to do, Karina whispered in my ear, saying, "Touya, give her a once-over with your divine sight."

"Hm?"

I did as I was told...and noticed a small orb inside Luna's chest. It was roughly the size of a golf ball. At a glance, I could tell it was a mutant core. That was the source of her new powers. That meant all I had to do was take it out...

"**[Apport]**."

I used my matter transfer spell to pluck the core out into my hand. Then, I threw it on the ground and stomped it to pieces. With the destruction of the core, Luna would have no more link to the wicked god's muddy divinity.

"That's fine, then. You guys can take her away now."

"At your command!"

Rebecca started dragging Luna to the dungeon, while the guards pushed the giant Viola popsicle along after her. That was certainly quite frightening... I had no idea what I would've done if Moroha and Karina hadn't been around.

That reminded me...if Bastet had come through, the puretree in Isengard had one less defender.

It was a bit early, but I decided to call Est of the Red Cats, since I knew there was no way Nia was awake.

"You never said it'd be this early. We'll be charging you extra for this!"

"Yeah, yeah... You greedy little..."

Nia stuck her tongue out at me. She was here, along with Est, Euni, Euri, and several other members of the Red Cats.

Gollem-wise, we had Rouge, Est's Akagane, and three Gollems I didn't recognize. They were all painted red, though. That suggested they were just general Red Cat Gollems.

"I need you to defend the puretree. We'll be sending reinforcements later on, but you guys are basically the first wave."

"Very well. We'll handle the job with care," Est said and nodded to me before heading through the mirror. I passed through with them.

CHAPTER II: PREPARING FOR THE SHOWDOWN

We came out into a forested area. Anubis, who stood nearby, came running over. The dog-like Gollem started sniffing around my legs like an abandoned puppy.

"Waaah! Grand Duke! You're okay?! Is the castle okay?! Is Sis okay?! Those jerks entered the mirror, but I had my orders to stay here, so... Auuugh!"

"It's all right. Everything's gonna be okay. Bastet got a little banged up, but it's nothing serious. You can head back now if you want. Good job."

"I can?! Thank you, thank youuu!" Anubis roared and charged through the mirror, his role now complete.

Albus was nearby as well, guarding the tree dutifully.

"Wow, it really did get kinda big."

I looked up at the puretree. It was around five meters tall. I was glad to see it was growing well enough.

I noticed a glowing substance coming out of the branches, presumably the magical particles.

"So all we gotta do is look after this tree?"

"Yeah. There's a good chance mutants are gonna come for it, so let me get some Frame Gears o— Oww..."

As I spoke, I was hit by a wave of nausea and fell to one knee.

Crap... I thought I'd be fine, but it seemed like the purification range was still a touch too small. It was definitely better than my previous exposure, but the effects of the divine venom were stronger based on the intensity of a person's divinity. Given that my divinity stemmed from God Almighty himself... Well...it was pretty effective on me.

I was still just a god-in-training, so I didn't have any way of resisting it yet...

"H-Hey, you okay? Are you sick?"

"Gh... I'm okay... Just... Hh... **[Gate]**."

I opened up a portal, making the Red Cat Chevaliers, Est's Red Lynx, and Nia's Tiger Rouge appear. Then, I looked over at the mechs before crawling over to the mirror.

"You guys can...h-handle the rest from here... C'mon, Albus."

"Affirmative."

I passed through the mirror and was immediately relieved of my symptoms. I hadn't quite fainted, but I was hit with a sense of fatigue.

"[Refresh]."

My fatigue was washed away by my spell, but I still felt a bit groggy. Almost like having a hangover... Not that I knew what that felt like, since I wasn't old enough to drink alcohol. Yeah, not old enough.

I felt a little better after resting for a bit, but it didn't improve my health too much. The purification range needed to be wider. The puretree could absorb more of the venom in proportion to its increased size. So eventually, it'd be big enough to purify all of Isengard. We just had to hold out against the mutants until then.

"Hey, Albus... How many mutants attacked during your watch?"

"Fifty-three. All were Lesser Constructs."

That...was certainly quite a lot... Maybe I'd need to send reinforcements to Nia earlier than I'd expected.

I whipped out my smartphone and looked up the numbers for Norn and Robert.

Apparently, the mutants attacked the puretree several times that day. Luckily, the Frame Gears were able to beat them back easily at each attempt.

Est reported the details to me over the phone. Even though the divine venom interfered with my magic, it didn't do anything about our phone reception, so that was a relief.

The puretree had been growing steadily and was already far taller than the trees in the surrounding area. Unfortunately, that meant it was no longer concealed, so the attacking mutants would likely increase as a result.

I'd sent Norn and Noir, along with Robert and Blau, to the forest as well. They'd taken their Over Gears, Leo Noir and Deer Blau, with them. Since I'd been to the area, all I had to do was open up a [Gate] to send people through. That made things simpler.

We had three crowns on the defensive team, so I couldn't imagine standard foes doing anything to them. Plus, Robert's Deer Blau could use its space-warping powers to negate any attacks that were done directly to the puretree.

"When will we be attacking?"

"Mm... It's a gut feeling here, but two more days. I think that's how much longer it'll take."

"Then we'll be on standby until then? How troublesome..." Hilde said as she dabbed her sweaty brow with a hand towel.

I agreed with her, but I didn't want to endanger any of my fiancees. If I'd charged us all in yesterday, we'd have definitely died. My fiancees also had the blessings of the divine in them, though not quite to my extent. I knew that they'd be strongly harmed by the divine venom. No matter how talented you were with a blade, you could still be beaten by a novice if you were drunk or incapacitated.

...Well, I did know one swordswoman who would probably win even if she was drunk, but that wasn't an option in this case. Plus, the effect of the divine venom on her would have been near-lethal, given her status... It was a pretty bad example in general.

Even Nia's team in Isengard were suffering small effects from the venom because of their relationship with me. They'd definitely be feeling like their physical states were slightly deteriorated compared to usual. The venom was practically the saying, "If you hate a priest, then you will come to hate his vestments" personified.

The more the puretree grew, the more it'd be able to spread its purification effects out across Isengard. And once it grew big enough, we could start our offensive.

The final battle was drawing near... As I thought about that inevitability, I received a call from Doc Babylon.

"'Sup, Doc?"

"Touya. The event we predicted has come to pass. A new type of mutant has appeared in Isengard."

A new type...? No way...

"Crap...!"

I went to the research laboratory and looked at the monitor display. I was shocked beyond belief. We'd seen it coming a while ago, but actually seeing it happen made it feel more real.

The monitor displayed a live feed from the Frame Gears under Nia's command. I saw several mutants that looked like salamanders, but the one I was staring at was very different.

A muddy-gold glow emanated from its body. It had two arms, two legs, and a head. It was humanoid in shape, but it wasn't a Dominant Construct... It looked just like a Frame Gear, even down to the size. It even wielded a dirty gold sword and shield for good measure.

"It's a Frame Gear mutant..."

"Based on the Chevalier they took during the last fight, I'm sure. Though, there are a few design tweaks here and there..." Doc Babylon grumbled as she took her e-cig out of her mouth.

It was somewhat similar to a Chevalier, that much was true. But it felt kind of different too... It was hard to describe, but it seemed more like a warped version of our designs. The color was different, sure, but even if it was the same color as a Chevalier, you'd be able to tell it wasn't one.

"But why? Why did they bother making a Frame Gear mutant? If they wanted a humanoid shape, then a cyclops or troll would've been far more effective."

She was right. If they wanted something robotic, then they had tons of Gollems to capture and observe in the past. They were already metallic enough due to their coloration, so it couldn't have been for some aesthetic reason either... Why had they bothered capturing a Frame Gear?

"Even if they aren't usually mechanical— Hm?"

Est's Red Lynx had sliced the Frame Gear mutant in half along the chest. It clattered to the ground.

"Oh... Now I see."

"You do? 'Cause I sure don't."

I would've appreciated it if she'd shared her wisdom sooner.

"It's harder to destroy something the smaller it is."

"...Huh?"

"Listen, Touya. The mutants and the Phrase have a common weak point no matter what kind of construct they are, right? They die if their core is destroyed. You know that much, yes?"

I nodded. She was stating the obvious.

"And you know the size of the core increases proportionally to the size of the creature, don't you?"

I nodded again. Lesser Constructs had small cores that were between the size of a baseball and a softball, Intermediate Constructs had cores that were between the size of a basketball and a balance ball, and Upper Constructs had cores that were between two and three meters in diameter. Dominant Constructs only had cores that were around the size of a cherry, though.

That showed that the size of the core didn't represent the strength of the creature, just its physique.

"So, looking at our Frame Gear impostor here...how big a core do you think it has?"

"If I were to guess...uhhh...it's around the size of an Intermediate Construct, so this big?"

I held out my hands as if I were cradling an invisible basketball. However, Doc Babylon shook her head, much to my surprise.

"You're wrong, Touya. It's this big," she said as she held out two fingers and measured a distance of about two centimeters between them.

"But that's tiny!"

"Look on the monitor, by the Red Lynx's feet. What do you see there?"

I squinted slightly at the screen, looking at the crumbled golden debris that had already started reforming. Before long, the reassembled pieces took the form of a tiny golden Skeleton.

"Huh?!"

"I must admit, I'm impressed. The Frame Gear mutant and the golden Skeleton are effectively one being. The Skeleton serves as the pilot and the core. See? The Skeleton reformed, so now the Frame Gear part is reforming as well. Looks like it can regenerate just as fast no matter how small the core is, and if we don't destroy the Skeleton, the Frame Gear will just keep coming back."

That made sense. But the Skeleton's core was only around the size of a marble. It'd be incredibly hard for the lumbering Frame Gears to take it out... Though, they could probably just stomp really hard.

I called up Est and told her what I'd just learned.

A few moments later, on the monitor, I saw her Red Lynx stomp hard on the little Skeleton as it tried to get back inside the mutant cockpit. When the Skeleton crumbled, so too did the Frame Gear, melting into viscous sludge. It was just as Doc Babylon had predicted.

"Hmm... This is a pain in the butt. The imposter Frame Gears... Uh, hm... I think I'll just call them Fake Gears. But yeah, the fakes seem linked to their Skeleton pilots and don't have minds of their own. It's just like Frame Gears and their own pilots, though our Frame Gears won't melt into goop if their pilots die!"

"So if we want to take out one of the fakes, we need to go for the cockpit?"

I could probably use [**Apport**] to pull the core out, but that spell required me to have a line of sight with my target... I'd have to use my divine sight if I wanted to do that.

"It's probably easiest to do what the Red Lynx just did. Knock the Skeleton out and stomp on it. Either that or completely obliterate the cockpit in one go."

Leen's Grimgerde could probably do it with its vulcan weaponry, but Elze's Gerhilde, Yae's Schwertleite, or Hilde's Siegrune couldn't.

Stomping the cockpit after knocking it down was probably easiest.

"Seems like we've got one more thing to worry about..."

"No, I don't think so. Look there."

The monitor showed other members of the Red Cats dealing with new Fake Gears, but they were fighting using their swords and shields. Something felt off.

"Have you noticed? The Fake Gears don't morph their bodies to attack. Normal mutants would've shifted their limbs into blades, stuff like that."

Huh, now that she mentions it, I do see that... They're regenerating, but they're not using their bodies offensively like the others... Why not?

"It's possible that morphing is a skill dependent on core size in relation to the body. The golden Skeleton's core is too small for the Fake Gear, so it can't draw out enough power to morph."

That made sense to me. The Skeleton's core could probably only morph the Skeleton at best, so the fakes might have actually turned out to be even weaker opponents than regular mutants.

I saw a Chevalier on the monitor slice a Fake Gear in half. It then stomped on the fallen mutant's upper body a few times, which made it fade away into slime and black smoke.

"Hm... This doesn't feel all that chivalrous..."

"Chivalry on the battlefield gets you dead. Fight to win."

Fair enough... It just feels a little awkward, since it's basically hitting an enemy while it's down... I know it's not exactly like that, but still! I watched a little longer, until all the mutants had been taken care of. The Chevaliers then sheathed their blades.

My smartphone started vibrating. It was Nia.

"Yep?"

"Hey, dumbass! You gonna just sit there and watch us starve?! We don't have any food with us, and there's no game to hunt!"

"Oh, I forgot about that..."

"YOU WHAT?!"

"No, I mean like...I did prepare some provisions, but I forgot to send them. Wait a bit and I'll get them to you."

That was definitely my fault. You couldn't battle on an empty stomach. When fighting on the frontier, rations often meant the difference between life or death. That being said, distance wasn't really an issue in our case.

I looked around for a clear space in the research laboratory... But there were bits of paper, scrap parts, and tools all over the place. It was no good. And so, I headed out into a nearby hallway and pulled Crea and Lu's homemade treats out from my **[Storage]**. I also took out some refreshments and a little bit of booze. Since they'd been stored in my own little pocket of space-time, the food was piping hot and the drinks were freezing cold.

"Hey, don't start chowing down! This stuff isn't for you!"

"Don't be a buzzkill, Touya. I'm just vibing. I haven't eaten all day."

Before I could react, Doc Babylon was munching away on some of the fried rice. She had a spoon sticking out of her mouth.

"**[Gate]**."

The portal spread out under the food, and it sank away slowly. If all had gone well, the food should have arrived right by Nia's group in Isengard.

I got a quick call from Est, who expressed her gratitude. I didn't mind, since I'd factored this into the expenses from the very beginning. It was almost time to start sending out our knights, anyway.

I headed over to the knight dorm and called out the volunteers. We could hardly leave the country without any of its knights, so only about half of the order would be joining this expedition.

I decided to send over fifty of the knights, with Nikola in command.

"This is a basic tent and some foodstuff. I've reduced its size, but if you use the term 'release' over there, it'll expand. Be sure to keep in regular contact with us, and report in if any of your men start feeling unwell."

"Understood. We'll be off, then."

I'd handed over a tiny dice-sized container to Nikola. In reality, it was a [Prison] I'd formed to store their supplies. I'd also included supplies for Nia's group in there.

Nikola popped the little cube into his pocket and turned to address the knights.

"All right, men! Time for our expedition!"

The knights clambered into their Chevaliers, while Nikola hopped into his Knight Baron. Nikola had the fully developed flight gear equipped on his Knight Baron in shield mode. That would help us if any flying mutants showed up.

I opened up a massive portal, and the Frame Gears marched through it to Isengard.

"I'll be off then, Grand Duke," Nikola spoke through his Frame Gear's speakers before departing through the portal.

"And they're off... I wanted to go as well..." Norn, or rather, Nore, grumbled quietly as her tail and ears twitched.

"If both of my sub-commanders leave for foreign lands, then who will step up to the plate here, hm?" Commander Lain was quick to lecture her.

"I mean, that's true, but...y-you're going later too, aren't you, Lain?! I'm the only one who has to stay! It's no fair!"

"Be that as it may, it was the grand duke's decision..."

Hey, hey... I want no part in this. I can't bring all three of you over there. Two's a stretch as-is! We've got Baba and Yamagata staying here too, but they're not technically knights...

"I'm sorry, Nore. But bear with it. It might not be enough to make up for it, but I'll give you and all the other knights here special daily desserts until Nikola's group gets back, okay?"

"Ohhh?! Daily?! You should've said so! Gimme pudding! Pudding a la mode!" Nore's exclaimed as her tail began swishing around like crazy. Her body was startlingly honest.

"E-Erm… Could I get some of that dessert…before I leave, perhaps?" Lain quietly mumbled as she fidgeted her hands. She was surprisingly honest too. I didn't really want to get in her bad books, so I decided it'd be fine.

We'll be making our forward base tomorrow when I send in the knights from the other countries… Gonna be pretty important. And once we've established the base, the march begins.

Genroku Era… Year Fifteen… Month Twelve… Day Five…

The Yamaga-ryu war drums ring out into the night, shaking the atmosphere within Edo. We forty-seven ronin must claim the head of Kira Yoshinaka in order to soothe the regrets of our late lord, Asano Takumi-no-Kami Naganori.

…Now certainly wasn't the time to indulge in the story of the forty-seven ronin. Plus, I didn't really want to relate our situation to Asano Takumi-no-Kami's, since he was forced to commit seppuku and disembowel himself… If that wasn't tempting fate, I had no idea what was.

Well, I could at least hope that we'd return without any casualties like the forty-seven ronin…who ended up killing themselves afterward. Never mind. My comparison was definitely not working well at all.

Anyway, I just wanted us all to get home safe. I shrugged a bit and headed to the kitchen to pick up the desserts I'd promised.

"...Time we got going, then," I said as I walked through the [Gate] and set foot in Isengard.

Yumina, Sue, Elze, Linze, Yae, Hilde, Sakura, Lu, and Leen all passed through alongside me. Paula toddled along too, of course. We all gazed up at the puretree.

The sight was something to behold.

"Well?"

"Mmm... I don't feel anything, so I think we're good."

"I do not feel anything strange, I do not."

Elze and Yae did a small warm-up motion as they confirmed their status. Nobody else felt ill or tired, either. I didn't really know why Paula was testing her range of motions, given she'd be completely fine, but it wasn't really an issue...

I certainly felt no ill effects. A minor sense of nausea hit me, but it was just the kind of feeling you'd get after eating something funky. That meant the purification was coming along nicely. I had a feeling that my sisters needed to stay back a bit longer, though.

"Wow... It sure is big!" Sue exclaimed as she stared up at the puretree with amazed eyes. It certainly didn't resemble the tiny sapling I had originally sent over. In fact, it was now so big that I had to crane my neck. I wondered just how many meters into the sky it stretched.

It was far beyond the size of our Frame Gears, even… Plus, it gave off an intimidating atmosphere, making it clear that it was the grandest tree in the forest.

"The sparkling is nice…"

"It is…"

Sakura and Linze looked at the magic particles being released from the puretree's leaves, which were quite beautiful.

"Grand Duke, miladies. This way." Nikola, who had come here earlier, came to meet us by the tree.

We entered the command tent that they'd set up, only to be greeted by various commanding officers from countries around the world. Our own commander, Lain, was also present.

There were no tense discussions or frantic arguments. The atmosphere was quite relaxed overall. They were all just sipping tea and making casual conversation with each other. I was a bit surprised, honestly. That being said, the moment I entered the tent, they all stood to attention.

"What's the situation?"

"No problems so far, really. Those Frame Gear constructs, er… Fake Gears? They've been attacking us fairly frequently, but they're few in number, so we've been beating them back on a rotational schedule," Belfast's deputy general, Neil, spoke up. The vice-commander of Lestia, Franz, also came over to talk shortly after that.

"We were concerned about Upper Constructs going on the offensive, however…"

"Oh, right. I don't think there'll be any Upper Constructs coming all the way out here. They definitely won't show up out of nowhere like they used to, at least."

"Oh? Why's that?"

"The Upper Constructs we've fought so far popped in from a space between worlds. That's why they cropped up in random locations during previous battles. We detected their emergence point and then hosted the battle in that area to intercept them. Basically, they can't pick and choose where they emerge, it was just wherever they happened to come out. But now the mutants attacking us are ones that you could consider native to Isengard. If they attacked us, they wouldn't be coming in from a space between worlds, they'd have to physically walk across the land to reach us."

I did not doubt that they'd come from the direction of that golden palace near Isenberg. The Upper Constructs were massive, so they moved pretty slowly in general. Not to mention the fact that Bastet had left a surveillance drone on the giant tower in Isenberg, which was set to notify us well in advance if something that large came lumbering in our direction.

The enemy might have been sending Fake Gears over in quick succession because they knew sending an Upper Construct was pointless.

"That being said, we can't slack off. We'll need to keep regular perimeter patrols, and send out scouts as well."

"Aye. We've got the Red Cats doing just that, so you needn't worry," Lain spoke clearly, but I was a bit surprised Nia's group had decided to take on that role. I had a feeling they'd probably ask for extra compensation later…

"They actually asked for something in exchange. They wanted you to create a bathhouse once you arrived," Nikola continued speaking as if reading my mind.

Pssh, extra compensation later? Never mind, they want it right now!

"A bathhouse, huh? I mean, that's not a bad idea... I get why you'd want that if you're over fighting for so long."

"This is a fairly humid place, so it's hard for sweat to even form to begin with."

"I guess that's fair... We do have a lot of female knights, so I should take their hygiene and cleanliness into account..."

Ugh, fine... I'll make it... The commanders and sub-commanders of the other nations also expressed their support for the idea, so I decided to finish building a public bath before dinner. It'd be harder for them if they couldn't sweat off the heat.

"We'll help with the cooking, then!"

Yumina, Lu, and Sue trotted off to the canteen tent.

"We will participate in the battle, we will."

Yae, Hilde, and Elze called their Valkyries from their [Storage]-enchanted rings, then charged off to the battlefield.

"As for us, we'll erect a barrier around the camp. There aren't just mutants here, after all."

Leen, Linze, and Sakura flew off on Linze's Helmwige. Considering the fact that the divine venom would affect them if they strayed too far, I couldn't imagine they'd be erecting a very large barrier.

All that was left was for me to make a bathhouse. Mixed bathing didn't really sound too relaxing, so I decided to separate by sex.

I walked a bit into the forest and looked for a suitable spot... I was pretty spoiled for choice, to be honest. The battles in the area had wrecked so many trees that most of the area was usable. I sighed quietly and started to clear the fallen tree trunks.

"This'll do, I think."

I dug a large pit for the bath using Earth magic. I'd already made a public bath at the Silver Moon in the past, which gave me knowledge of how to make the proper pipes and drainage system.

Well...there are a lot of guys here... Guess I'll make the male bath a bit bigger. I'll pay a bit more attention to the female bath, though... Don't really want them fussing about it not being up to scratch later...

"All righty, time to get to work."

I rolled my sleeves back and started chopping some nearby fallen trees. I'd decided to recycle them into materials for the bathhouse.

"Ooh, looks great! Real home-like! Good job, Touya!" Nia, who'd just returned with the other Red Cats, said that as she looked at the public baths with glee.

That's right! Go ahead and praise me a bit more, why don't you? I worked hard here!

"Oh, but wait... Since it's an open bath, wouldn't the whole place be visible from a Frame Gear cockpit?" Est raised a fair point as she glanced upward from the open-air bath. She was right, but luckily, I'd already created a solution.

"There's a special kind of visual magic I've enchanted the entire bathhouse with. When someone's in the bath, the whole place looks like a mass of trees from anywhere other than the entrance. It's all good."

The girls were clearly suspicious of my words, since they all went and confirmed that by themselves. And just like I said, they only ended up seeing a mass of reddish-orange, leafy trees. I didn't like the idea of them thinking I had ulterior motives, to be honest.

"This isn't some setting you can toggle on or off, right?"

"Obviously not! If I tried to pull something like that, my life would be in danger," Norn, who'd come along with Noir, asked me that ridiculous question. Did she think I was suicidal or something? If I pulled something like that with my fiancees so close by, I'd be done for.

"If you're still worried even after all that, I have towels available. There are also some swimsuits."

This wasn't like a hot spring back on earth. It was fine if they wanted to wear stuff in the bath. After all, I'd enchanted the place so [Clean] triggered every so often.

"...Why exactly do you have so many female swimsuits just ready to go, anyway...?"

"Yeah... I was wondering the same..."

"Well, you guys have fun! See ya!"

I dashed away before Euni and Euri asked any more weird questions.

Don't get the wrong idea! They just got mixed into a batch I got from Fashion King Zanac! I didn't buy them specifically or anything!

The area around the puretree had become a fully established garrison. There were tents scattered around, and knights walking about. It was pretty unusual to see knights from different countries fraternizing so casually. I saw some arguing, some talking about their homes, and there were even a few hitting on some women together.

A lot of the knights from the eastern side of the world were showing knights from the former Reverse World how to ride Frame Gears properly. But even so, this place was on the edge of a battlefield. Sometimes, the sounds of Frame Gears clashing against mutants could be heard in the distance.

I entered one of the nearby tents.

"Any news?"

"Negative. Mutants are attacking as usual, but they're just mutants from the surrounding area. There is no reaction at all from the golden palace," Cesca, still wearing her maid uniform, turned from a monitor and removed her comms headset to reply.

"Do ya think they've noticed us yet?"

"I, like, totally think that's the case, yes. They should be aware by now that the divine venom is disappearing in this area."

Rosetta and Monica muttered amongst themselves as they stared at the monitor. The monitor showed a feed from the surveillance camera drone we'd set up at Isenberg's tower. The creepy sight kind of gave off a bad Zombie B-movie vibe, but it was a bunch of golden Skeletons instead of Zombies.

"They may be coming up with a plan, you see."

Flora had a point. They very well could have been biding their time. Our enemies had to know what would happen if we were left unchecked, so I couldn't imagine them not retaliating.

"Just keep up the surveillance for the time being. Rosetta, Monica, you two handle Frame Gear maintenance."

"Aaah... Stern as ever, sir!"

"She isn't incorrect. You should, like, totally let us watch some anime as a reward. I wanna watch some anime and stuff!"

I sighed a bit and gave in to the demands of the booing duo. I said I'd let them watch a mecha anime after all this was done. They kind of forced me into it, but it wasn't really that big of a compromise for me. The two of them then bolted out of the tent with smiles on their faces.

"Master, if you're giving out rewards, then I'd like a hardcore S&M maid—"

"Enough out of you, you demented gynoid."

I glared over at Cesca, who was looking at me and breathing heavily. She was much harder to deal with than the rest.

After that, I called over Ende from Brunhild, since I figured the environment was tolerable enough for him at this point. I felt a little bad, though, since he'd probably get a bit sick. He was Uncle Takeru's beneficiary, so he obviously had some divine blessing in him, but I needed him on the front lines.

He was also the one I was counting on to deal with that Phrase General, Xeno.

After I ended the call on my smartphone, I opened up a [Gate] to pull him through. Ende walked right on over, followed by Melle, Lycee, and Ney. The three Phrase girls were in their human disguises, since I didn't want to cause a ruckus.

"Yo. You called us in sooner than I thought. Are we charging them?"

"No, not yet. I just wanted you guys on hand just in case."

Ende seemed a bit puzzled, but I caught him up to speed. Originally, I'd given him the impression they'd be coming in a bit later, but that was my bad.

"Oooh, what a lovely scent!"

"Lady Melle, this must be curry!"

"Oh... I smell fried pork... It must be katsu curry."

As I spoke with Ende, the three girls zeroed in on the pleasant scent in the area. Even I wasn't sure the smell was katsu curry, so I was a bit frightened by how adept their senses were. Lu was probably making it in the cafeteria. Given that she had divine taste buds, I had a feeling she was making an incredible dish.

"I've set a tent aside for you guys already. You can basically do whatever you want until the battle starts, but try not to get into any arguments."

"I got it. Oh right, Touya... Sorry and all, but can you..."

"...Cafeteria's down in that direction."

"Yeah. Sorry, the girls will be restless until they've eaten a bit... Okay, ladies, we'll head to the— Huh?!" Ende turned around and found that the three girls were already well on their way to the cafeteria tent.

"H-Hey! Wait up!" Ende roared, running after them in a panic.

...You know, Ende...when I first met you, you had this stoic and mysterious air about you. You were super cool, actually. I kinda thought you might be a credible threat to me if I got on your bad side. When did you turn into comic relief? Same goes for the rest of them, really. But I guess because I got to know them, they've become a lot more human in my eyes.

I watched the four of them run off before I heard the sound of a mechanical whirring and looked overhead. Linze's Helmwige was above, lowering itself slightly. Sakura and Leen jumped out of the cockpit, while Paula just kind of fell out.

...P-Paula? Your neck's bent at a weird angle... I know you're a stuffed toy, but are you sure you're okay?

Linze's Helmwige had a wide cockpit, since it contracted during the transformation sequence. As such, there was room for the two girls (and a stuffed toy) in the rear seats.

"We've set up several barriers. There shouldn't be any magical beasts near the camp, now."

"There were some flying mutants as well... We shot them down..."

"We? I was the only one doing any shooting," Linze hopped down and cut in after Sakura.

"There are dozens of Fake Gears headed our way from Isenberg. They'll probably be here in around thirty minutes or so."

"Copy that. I'll be sure to relay the info. Thanks again, girls."

I heard Linze's basic report, then opened up my smartphone map. The map had previously been blocked by the divine venom, but now it was usable because the atmosphere was less saturated with it.

"Run search. Use my location as the focal point. Find all mutants and Fake Gears."

"Searching... Search complete. Displaying."

The map ended up being projected into the air. It showed that there were quite a few enemies left. We needed to defend the puretree until Moroha and the others could come through to take over defense, and we could begin our attack on the palace.

I decided to ask Ende to help in his Dragoon. It was time to fight.

"[Gladius]!"

Forty-eight glimmering projectiles attacked all the Fake Gears around me. The daggers busted the cockpits, then went after the golden Skeletons that had fallen out from inside.

"Sphere mode."

The daggers transformed into spheres and began to crush the Skeletons to bits. The [Gravity]-infused spheres managed to pulverize the Skeletons along with their cores in no time flat, melting my foes into mush alongside their Fake Gears.

"They're more annoying to deal with than regular mutants, but I'm glad we don't need to trace their cores or anything."

I sighed quietly from inside Reginleif's cockpit as I watched some of our Chevaliers smashing a few Fakes Gears with battlehammers. Hammer-based weapons were more effective, since they could smash the Skeletons inside with the raw blunt force trauma.

"Run search. All purified territory within Isengard."

"Search complete. Displaying."

My cockpit projected a map of Isengard with the purified areas displayed in blue. The red areas were places that were still steeped in divine venom.

The map showed that the purification zone had reached the golden palace, which basically meant we didn't have to worry about the venom anymore. Now all I needed to do was call Moroha and the others to have them defend the puretree, then begin my march on the enemy.

I hopped out of Reginleif, contacted Moroha, and used [Gate] to bring the group through. Moroha, Takeru, and Karina all flexed and stretched after walking through the portal.

"Mmm. I don't feel like I'm at my best, but it'll do."

"You can still feel the venom? I thought we'd purified most of it."

Moroha worried me a bit, which made Takeru and Karina laugh.

"It's just because this whole territory is connected to parts that are steeped in the venom. We're in our human forms, but we're still full gods. That makes us sensitive to even the tiniest bit of atmospheric impurity. Don't sweat it, though. It won't actually hurt us. Just makes us a little queasy at worst."

"Aye aye! I got guts to power through, no big deal! Leave this to us, and you go do your mission, kid! God Almighty is watching from home, don't forget it!"

It seemed like they'd be fine, thankfully. All three of them gave me a motivational pat on the back. I knew that the puretree would be completely safe in the hands of the trio, so I just had to make sure that the rest of my mission went off without a hitch.

I pulled out a greatsword and a longsword for Moroha from [Storage], then a bow, quiver, and hand-axes for Karina. Lastly, I pulled out the same kind of gauntlets Ende was wearing and gave them to Takeru. All the weapons were made of crystal. I'd even made sure that Takeru's gauntlets were the same design as Ende's, which I had a feeling he'd appreciate. Probably, at least… The moment they took up their weapons, they charged off to the battlefield. They really ran off quickly, so they must've been itching to fight.

It was pretty amazing that they were going up against Fake Gears without anything other than their weapons and bodies, but I knew that they'd be capable of handling it.

After all that, I threw Reginleif into [Storage] and headed back to my fiancees.

"Are we heading out, are we?"

"Indeed, is it time?"

The moment I entered the tent, Yae and Hilde stood up. Yae had her blade in hand, and Hilde was wielding the crystal blade I'd given her on our first meeting. Seemed like they were itching to go too.

"It's time. I called Moroha and the others out, so the puretree's fine now. We just need to advance on the forest and take out the wicked god."

Everyone nodded at once. None of them looked the least bit apprehensive. I was pretty amazed by their calm attitudes, but part of me was worried, since I felt like I was the only concerned person there.

I called up Ende's group and told Commander Lain that we'd be beginning our mission at any moment.

"Very well, Grand Duke. I wish you the greatest of luck."

"Thanks. We'll be off, then."

I opened up a **[Gate]** that took me and the others to Isenberg, the former capital. The ones joining me on this mission were my fiancees, Ende, Melle, Ney, and Lycee. It was a grand total of fourteen people. Sadly, Paula had to stay behind.

As we stepped through the portal, the scene that unfolded around us stunned us into silence. The place was positively desolate. Dark clouds loomed overhead, and corpses piled up in the streets. The city that was once the witch-king's greatest achievement was no more. Isenberg was basically just a mass grave.

"I'd heard the stories, but seeing it in the flesh is awful..." Elze shook her head quietly.

Bastet's report indicated that the corpses had no physical signs of damage, and that was definitely true. The only proof of their exposure to the elements was their worn-down clothing. Each one of them had died with expressions of twisted agony and grief on their faces. It was a little unsettling just to look at...

"Touya!"

"Huh?"

I turned in response to Linze's shout and saw a man charging toward me. A man who had been a prone corpse mere moments ago. His tongue lolled out of his mouth, and his eyes were perfect whites. He was the spitting image of a Zombie, and I was honestly frightened.

"[Slip]!"

"Gruuugh!"

The Zombie slipped, moaned, and fell face-first into the ground.

Geez, that was freaky. It's scary as hell when you're attacked out of nowhere.

Linze didn't skip a beat, casting [**Fire Storm**] on the Zombie. It was consumed by the swirling flames and burned to ashes... Or at least, that was what I thought before a golden Skeleton emerged from the inferno.

"I knew it. Those who have their souls sucked out are fated to become these golden Skeletons. Look at its chest," Leen spoke up, and I glanced over at the Skeleton's ribcage. There was a mutant core nestled inside, around the size of a golf ball. This body had already become a mutant, well and truly.

"Lestian Sacred Sword: Fifth Swirl!" Hilde roared and plunged her blade into the Skeleton's chest. Her rotating strike shattered both the Skeleton's ribs and the core they were housing.

The Skeleton melted into nothingness, letting out black smoke as it vanished. It was likely that they'd been building their Skeleton army from the dead here.

"We've raised a bit of a fuss, Touya."

"Hm?"

Ende's comments made me turn around, and I noticed that all the corpses in the vicinity were now shambling toward us. It was gross.

"Will purification magic work on them?"

"On ordinary Zombies, yes... But these ones are just Crystal Skeletons wearing skin...so I doubt it would do a thing."

"Hmph..." Sue seemed unsatisfied with Leen's response. She was probably annoyed because she could've easily wiped out an undead horde with her light spells.

Sakura used [**Icebind**] to freeze the feet of the approaching Zombies. This allowed Leen to cast her own spell as a follow-up.

"Burn forth, Wind! Gale of Flames: [Ignis Hurricane]!"

A massive whirlwind started blowing through the area, incinerating everything it touched. The spell Leen had unleashed was a compound spell she'd learned from Babylon's library.

It was truly a terrifying force, reducing the Zombies around us to Skeletons in an instant. But sadly, even powerful magic could do little more than burning away the flesh. Their bones still had the Phrase's anti-magic attributes, after all.

Luckily, we had Yae, Hilde, Lu, Elze, and Ende to make up for that. They charged in and started shattering cores. I didn't want to seem like I was just standing there, so I took a few potshots with Brunhild as well.

"Seems like all the corpses here are Skeletons, then."

"But why did they attack us? They hadn't moved at all before now..." Lu muttered to herself as she sheathed her blades. Much to my surprise, Ende came over with the answer.

"They operate similarly to the Phrase, so I'm willing to bet they reacted to our heartbeats. Look at Melle and the other Phrase girls. They haven't reacted to them at all, see?"

He was right. There were no golden Skeletons near that trio at all. Melle, Ney, and Lycee all had a small [**Prison**] enchanted around their cores that prevented sound from escaping. It was a countermeasure that prevented them from being detected by the other mutants. Their heartbeats, or rather, their wavelengths, weren't audible.

"Let me put it this way. If you walked past a group of magical beasts while playing loud musical instruments, they'd obviously wake up, right?"

131

He had a point. If someone woke me up by playing loud instruments, I'd probably want to attack them too.

"Well, let's not waste our time here. We should head to the palace."

I opened up [**Storage**] and pulled Reginleif out. Everyone else summoned their Frame Gears and climbed into the cockpits.

Ende's Dragoon was built for speed and maneuverability, so it didn't have much space in the cockpit. Melle managed to squeeze in with Ende, but Ney and Lycee had to ride outside on its hands. They could have easily ridden along with Linze in Helmwige, but the two of them said they wanted to stay as close to Melle as possible.

Linze and I took to the skies, hovering above the others as we began our march to the palace.

"Must be nice flying up there, Touya. Can't you upgrade my Dragoon so it can do that too?"

"Why not outfit yourself with one of our flight gears?"

"You kidding me? This is a machine built for speed! A big-ass shield like that would just slow me down... Guess it's a no-go, huh?"

I had nothing to say to Ende's grumbling. He was right. The ideas behind the Dragoon and the flight gear were fundamentally incompatible. The Dragoon was built for land speed, so it was pointless making it fly. My Reginleif was the culmination of Frame Gear tech, combining the knowledge gained from every different version we'd built, so I wasn't just about to let him have one too!

We headed out of Isenberg and came to a vast plain. The dark clouds in the sky blotted out the sun, making it seem like night had fallen despite it only being noon.

We carried on across the plains until we could see a muddy golden mass of giant crystals on the horizon. The fact that it was visible despite the distance meant it must have been massive...

It really did seem like some kind of palace. At that point, we decided to stop our advance in order to figure out our plan of action.

"Is there a chance they haven't noticed us yet?"

"They've definitely noticed us. The golden Skeletons that were surrounding the palace are inbound."

Yumina's words made me zoom in my camera, and I saw the mass of Skeletons making their way in our direction.

"Looks like it's my turn."

The black Frame Gear, Leen's Grimgerde, stomped forward.

"Guess it's war, eh? Might as well start it off with a bang!"

Grimgerde's chest armor slid open, revealing two Gatling guns. Two cannons atop its shoulders also slid forward and angled upward. The six-barreled Gatling gun on both arms began revving up, as did the head-mounted vulcan cannon and the sixteen-shot rocket pods on the shoulders and waist.

Grimgerde's heels dropped a deep anchor into the ground, fixing it firmly to one spot.

"Volley primed! Full Burst!" Leen yelled out, and a veritable storm of bullets went flying toward the approaching Skeleton army. Frame Gears couldn't technically run out of ammo, since they automatically replenished themselves using teleportation magic connected to the ammo storage on Babylon, so Grimgerde was more likely to overheat than anything.

The golden Skeletons were smashed to smithereens by the incoming projectiles. It was hard to say whether or not any of the bullets or rockets hit the Skeletons in their cores, since they were obliterated along with the landscape at their feet.

The Skeletons were blown sky-high, glimmering as they flew through the air in several pieces.

"That is certainly a bang, it is..."

"I can't believe it... It just keeps on firing..."

I was pretty amazed as well. It was basically a non-stop barrage of the [**Explosion**] spell. Plus, the power fluctuated depending on which type of ammo was being launched, so it was variable. I had a feeling that only Leen or I could sustain this kind of attack.

Shell after shell landed on the enemy, but the artillery fire showed no sign of stopping. Each explosive blast dug another chunk out of the ground, reshaping the plain's very landscape. This was the true power of Grimgerde, a Frame Gear that had been designed for overwhelming mass destruction.

After many long minutes, the hail of bullets came to an end. Grimgerde stopped moving entirely, and white smoke vented from every port on it.

Grimgerde's main weakness was that it needed to enter a cooldown period after unleashing an attack like that. The machinery would heat up to an extreme level, so the magic engravings would begin cooling the armor. Several blue lines ran across the black armor, generating more and more steam that rose upward and dissipated. The entire process took roughly twenty seconds, but Grimgerde was extremely vulnerable during that period.

That was why Leen never just used the full burst attack in regular battles. It could only be used when there were allies around to keep her safe, or if she was firing from a completely defended area.

When the smoke finally cleared, roughly ninety percent of the Skeletons were on the ground in fragmented chunks, dissolving into nothingness as black smoke plumed from their parts.

"Grand Duke… I hear something… Cracking and splitting… right ahead…from the crystal mass…"

Just as Sakura spoke, a crystal pillar broke off one of the golden palace's corners, and a group of Fake Gears came swarming out toward us from the massive hole. They were moving to our location at high speeds.

They all wielded dark gold weapons and moved in unison. Their synchronization was confusing to me, since I hadn't expected them to be so organized.

"Touya. Melle just registered General Xeno's wavelength. He's among that group."

"Seriously?"

Ende's words made me zoom my camera in on the group of Fake Gears. There were several spike-armored versions mixed in with the crowd, with an even more unique one among those. It was larger than usual and had a comb-like plume atop its head like a Roman helmet. It was likely the one that belonged to their commander.

"No doubt about it. Xeno is inside that one. And those spiked Fake Gears around him are likely being piloted by his subordinates from Phrasia. They're moving very differently from the others."

Just like that, a new enemy stood in our path. He was the Phrase's ultimate combat-oriented lifeform. The strongest of their species. General Xeno.

A high-pitched voice resonated across the battlefield. It was vocal magic being released by Sakura's Rossweisse. Her song had the effect of increasing all our agility when fighting against the enemy.

The French pop song rang out as we clashed against the Fake Gears.

I switched the twelve Fragarach boards on Reginleif's back to form an enormous lance.

"**[Accel Boost]!**" I roared as I charged ahead, my Frame Gear infused with my magic. Then, I speared Fake Gear after Fake Gear with my lance, charging through their ranks like Moses parting the Red Sea.

"Take this!" Sue, in her Ortlinde's Overlord form, said as she brought a hammer smashing down on incoming foes. It wasn't a throwing hammer this time, but a regular old warhammer. It wasn't anything special at all, just a huge hunk of metal that was only good for smashing. However, in the hands of the enormous Ortlinde Overlord, it was a brutal weapon of mass destruction.

The golden Skeleton pilots that had fallen from the Fake Gears I'd smashed were turned into paste by Sue's furious hammer attacks. Those that tried to get out of the way were trampled by Ortlinde's feet. It was an utter massacre; none of them managed to escape.

Sue's Ortlinde may have shimmered a similar gold to the Fake Gears, but it was clearly leagues ahead of them in terms of might.

"Hiyah!"

Ortlinde swung its hammer like a golf club, sending several Fake Gears flying into the distance. The airborne enemies were promptly dispatched with pin-point accuracy by Yumina's Brunnhilde. Thanks to her precision, we were able to press on without worrying about what was behind us.

"Gaaaaaah!"

Elze, presumably emboldened by the knowledge of that safety, had her Gerhilde charge into the enemy ranks and started brawling. At least, I hoped that was why she was being so reckless. Gerhilde shattered each and every Fake Gear that dared to step near it.

"SMASH!"

Gerhilde's fist smashed into one of the Fake Gear cockpits, following it up instantly with an [**Explosion**]-propelled pile bunker blast that completely annihilated the Skeleton inside. Just to be certain, Elze stomped on the fallen Skeleton fragments. It would've been a waste if the core survived, after all.

"Kokonoe Secret Style: Bee Stinger!"

"Lestian Sacred Sword: Fifth Swirl!"

The purple samurai and the orange knight stood back to back, shattering Fake Gear cockpits on either side of them. Yae masterfully handled her Schwertleite alongside Hilde's Siegrune. The two of them slashed foe after foe, staying back to back in perfect tandem. With each flash of their blades, more muddy-golden fragments fell to the ground.

Bullets flew in from afar to finish off the Skeletons in the wreckage. They were fired by Lu's Waltraute, which was equipped with the C-Unit for long-range engagement. The emerald-green Frame Gear launched payloads that exploded above the enemy, bursting into a shower of [**Gravity**]-enchanted phrasium fragments that rained down on the fallen foes. The attack worked much like the cluster attacks I employed against Upper Constructs in the past.

Leen's Grimgerde, which had recovered from its cooldown period, was launching similar attacks.

High up in the air, Linze's Helmwige soared across the battlefield. She was relaying real-time intelligence about battlefield changes to us. Linze was also casting [**Ice Wall**] from above, blocking off enemy groups as necessary, and luring them into traps. It was pretty amazing.

I looked to the side and saw Ende's Dragoon veering away from the battle. Of course, I knew that he wasn't fleeing. I could see that he was luring several of the stronger, spiked Fake Gears away with him.

Since I left the Phrase General Xeno to Ende's group, I released the [**Prison**] spell I'd placed around the three girls' cores. That effectively meant they were broadcasting their position to the mutants in the area.

Thus, Xeno would be able to see that the Sovereign was right before him. In effect, that turned them into bait. I was still a little worried about the size of the group Xeno had with him, though…

"Hey, Ende. Seems like you're pretty popular right now. You gonna be able to manage?"

"Pfft. Don't give me that, Touya. You're way more popular. But don't worry, the ones chasing us aren't mutants. They're Dominant Constructs, regular ones, just like Melle and the others. Pure Phrase from the homeworld."

That information confused me. I wondered if there was some reason they hadn't been converted.

"Elze, Sakura. Sorry for the trouble but can you lend Ende some help? Just stick to supporting him, don't charge in."

"Mmh… Fine… Guess I can help out my useless fellow disciple…"

"Are they slowing you down, Grand Duke…? They deserve to be reprimanded…"

"Touya… Your brides-to-be are a little bit…"

"A-A little what? W-Wonderful? I know!" I answered quickly, since Elze and Sakura were still on the line. I couldn't exactly say anything bad about them while they were in earshot!

There were about twenty of the spiked Fake Gears heading after Ende's Dragoon. Gerhilde and Rossweisse came up from behind them, hot on their tail.

I decided to entrust them with handling that situation, so I could focus on the battle at hand.

"This'll do," Ende proclaimed as he spun his Dragoon around, ready to face his pursuers head-on.

"Are you ready for this?"

"I am. Who else could put an end to this but me?"

Ende's lover, the Sovereign that once reigned at the apex of Phrasium life, nodded solemnly. And, after hearing her resolve, Ende didn't hesitate to press down on the button that opened the cockpit hatch.

The monitor in front of them rose upward, and dim, natural light shone down on to them both. Melle stood proudly atop the opened hatch, silently staring across the plain. Her visage was an imposing one, in all honesty. She shone with the majesty that suited the title of Sovereign. Ende couldn't help but think she was far more regal than a certain grand duke they both knew. She'd already removed the illusion pendant that she'd received from Touya. She chose to stare down the incoming enemies with her true body, with her ice-blue eyes.

Ney and Lycee, true to their roles as her personal guards, stood in their true forms as well. Each stood atop one of the Dragoon's hands, lying in wait.

Once the Fake Gears made it a certain distance from them, they stopped moving. Then, following suit with the Dragoon, the Fake Gear hatches opened as well. The comparatively tiny forms within were revealed to be crystal-clad beings of pure phrasium, Dominant Constructs.

The hatch of the largest Fake Gear opened up, revealing a much more imposing Phrase lifeform. He stood with his arms folded, prompting Melle and the others to narrow their eyes. He was a Dominant Construct with jagged, blood-red crystals clumped around his body. The Phrase were not a species that aged. They grew from cores, manifested a physical form, and at a certain point they reached maturity and no more physical changes came about. It wasn't too dissimilar to how elves and fairies aged.

The man who stood before Melle and the others looked to be in his early twenties if viewed through a human lens. His eyes were sharp and narrow, like those of a hawk. His face was plastered with an arrogant grin. Back on Phrasia, this powerful creature had served as general, leading countless Phrase soldiers into battle against their enemies. His name was Xeno.

"Been a while, Sovereign. You're looking plenty healthy."

"I am Sovereign no more. I don't need your false pleasantries, General... No, Xeno. Answer me this. Why did you leave Phrasia? I left you orders to stand by the new Sovereign's side, did I not?"

There was a fair bit of distance between the two, but communication didn't appear to pose any problems. It seemed that Dominant Constructs had some form of intuitive understanding in that regard.

The conversation extended to Ney, Lycee, and even Ende. The only ones who wouldn't be able to understand the conversation were Elze and Sakura. They'd have been able to hear that some kind of noise was being transmitted, but they'd fail to grasp the intricacies of the conversation.

"The next Sovereign, you say? Sorry to say it, ma'am. That little runt doesn't have what it takes. Hell, don't those two weaklings next to you agree? They left Phrasia to look for you, didn't they? It's only natural we wouldn't want our species to suffer under such weak rule."

Xeno's words prompted Ney and Lycee's ire. Just as Ney was about to speak up, Melle stopped her.

"You believe my younger brother to be weak, Xeno?"

"No shit. He was talking about things like peaceful cohabitation and making amends with our foes. Do you think such weak thoughts are appropriate for our species? If there's an enemy in your way, crush it. If they have some kind of use, then employ them as a tool. I can't even bear to entertain the thought of serving such a cowardly little priss. Fighting is in our cores, Sovereign. I can't serve one who rejects his base instincts," Xeno said with a grin on his face, but Melle remained composed.

He couldn't think of anything other than battle. He truly was Gila's brother in that regard. He was bred for war and thrived in war. Even if he didn't indiscriminately fight on a whim like his younger brother, they were philosophically similar people.

"To be honest, I was thinking about killing the little twerp. But I didn't really feel like that would be satisfying, you know? No fun in smushing an insect. That's when Yula showed up with a tempting little offer, you see. He told me he'd be able to prepare a situation where I could fight you, Sovereign. I gladly accepted. I didn't want anything to do with that weird golden shit, though."

"I see... So it was Yula pulling the strings all along. Where is he, anyway?"

"Beats me... Been a while since I've seen him, don't really give a shit. Enough prattling, Sovereign. It's time you quenched my thirst for battle," Xeno smiled wide as he said that, his carnivorous teeth flashing over the distance. He wasn't leaving without the fight he'd been craving.

"Very well. It seems further discourse would be wasted on you children. As the former Sovereign, I will take it upon myself to send you to the next life."

"Pah. Nice of you to finally attend to your duties properly," Xeno sneered, but gave a respectful bow nonetheless. He then returned to his cockpit.

Ende closed his cockpit and picked up a comm call from Elze.

"So? How'd the talk go?"

"Not so good, not that we were expecting a peaceful solution. Still, we wanted to know why they were here, and we found out. Now we can proceed as planned."

"Got it. I'll take out the ones on the outer rim, okay?"

"Go for it."

When Ende finished speaking, Sakura's singing voice rang out from Rossweisse's speakers. The song had a great, upbeat flow, it grooved through the battlefield in a jaunty manner. She was singing the song with its original lyrics, so nobody in the area had any idea what it was about. It was a famous song by an English pop duo, with lyrics like, "don't leave me hanging on like a yo-yo." The title was actually a bit different for its Japanese release, but it was still a great melody.

The song spurred the magical reactors inside the nearby Frame Gears and improved the agility of Sakura's allies by extension.

"Let's do this, Gerhilde!"

The crimson reaper charged into battle, kicking off from the ground as it activated its back-mounted boosters. Before anyone could blink, Gerhilde was right in the middle of the fray, smashing its mighty fist into a Fake Gear's cockpit.

The pile bunker came seconds afterward, driving through the enemy pilot and obliterating them entirely.

"That's one down!"

Another Fake Gear came in to fight Gerhilde, but it simply backed up and delivered a swift roundhouse kick in response. A blade popped out of Gerhilde's leg, bisecting the Fake Gear at the cockpit, and splitting the pilot in two.

"And that's two!"

Ende couldn't help but feel a sense of foreboding dread as he watched his fellow disciple gleefully smash the Dominant Constructs to bits.

"...W-Well, I guess it takes a very special kind of girl to match pace with Touya."

Ende thought all of Touya's fiancees were a little bit weird, but he certainly knew better than to say that out loud. He had a lot of sense in that regard. No matter the era or world he was in, angering a fair maiden a one-way ticket to getting your ass beat.

"All right, let's deal with our enemy."

Ende turned the Dragoon to face Xeno's Fake Gear head-on. Their enemy wielded a large sword and shield. He requested Ney and Lycee jump down from the Dragoon's hands, lest they get in the way.

"Hey, Endymion! If anything happens to Lady Melle, don't think I'll forgive you!"

"In the worst-case scenario, sacrifice yourself to save Lady Melle."

"Th-Thanks for the emotional support, guys... I appreciate it."

Ende slumped his shoulders slightly. Melle giggled softly and opened her mouth.

"Oh my, did you want them to cheer you on?"

"...Nah. Not quite, I guess. Your support's good enough for me, Melle."

"Hehe… Thank you, Ende. Do your best. You are my champion, after all. I'll be rooting for you."

"You can count on me."

The Dragoon released its heel anchors, prepared for a high-speed clash. The miniature magic motors in its leg began to whir, roaring like a dragon. Ende's precious machine was itching for a fight as well.

"Let's roll, Dragoon!"

The Dragoon, housing the Phrase Sovereign and the wanderer of worlds, charged forward at full power. The ground rushed by beneath their feet. The Dragoon accelerated even faster, thanks to the vernier thrusters on its waist and back.

The Dragoon drew two phrasium blades from its back, meeting General Xeno's muddy-gold broadsword head-on. A heavy clang rang out as the weapons clashed.

"Gh!"

Ende was stupefied. His weapons were made out of phrasium, and they'd been strengthened by Touya's absurd magic. The fact that Xeno had managed to parry his attack was baffling. He swung around with the second blade, but it was blocked by the muddy-gold shield. It was clearly made from the same material as the sword.

"That's no normal Fake Gear, is it?"

"Heh… Took you long enough. I made this thanks to Yula, even if it pains me to owe such a sniveling weasel a debt."

More interestingly than that, Ende couldn't help but notice the strange chi-like aura emanating from the sword and shield. He couldn't quite place it, but something was unsettling about the aura wrapped around that Fake Gear.

"…I don't remember being able to see energy so clearly before…" Ende mumbled to himself. He wondered if this was perhaps one of those traits, like the ones Touya's fiancees had.

If this was such a gift from the divine, he'd likely gotten it from his master. He couldn't be sure if he was happy about having that power or not, but he put it out of mind and backed up from the Fake Gear in front of him.

"Guess we should get him out of there first."

Ende charged forward full-throttle with his Dragoon, moving in to attack and then falling back, repeatedly. The Dragoon was built for this kind of speed-based offense. It would slowly get in small hits while looking for a chance to land a massive one.

"Baha! Pathetic! You think such half-assed attacks are gonna work?! You better learn to take this seriously!" Xeno screamed as his shield came rushing in toward the Dragoon's incoming weapon, bypassing it and striking the Frame Gear right on the arm.

The Dragoon was staggered due to the sudden impact, allowing Xeno to bring his massive blade down on to the mech's head.

"Gah!"

Ende just dodged the strike by a hair's breadth. He didn't escape fully unharmed, though. The blade had sliced off one of the mech's decorative horns. Ende remained crouched and switched the wheels on the bottom into reverse mode. He sped backward.

"You won't get away, brat!"

The Fake Gear being piloted by Xeno hurled its shield toward the retreating Dragoon. The projectile blasted forward and knocked one of the legs hard, shattering one of the wheels to bits.

"Ghah!"

The Dragoon completely lost its balance, tumbling to the ground. Xeno rushed in, wasting no opportunity, and brought his blade high into the air.

"Ghh!"

Ende raised his weapon up, straining hard against the weapon above. The Dragoon was more agile, but this meant that its body wasn't as sturdy as a standard Frame Gear. Unfortunately, a mech designed for speedy combat was in no state to hold its own up close against a powerful foe.

"What's wrong?! Is this all you have?! I want to fight even more!"

"Ghh... Doesn't matter if it's Gila or this guy... Fighting against the combat strain is rougher than it should be. Sorry, Melle... Can you lend me your strength?"

"Of course I can, Ende. This isn't just your battle. It's mine as well."

"Hm?!"

The Dragoon suddenly dropped its weapons. Icy crystals began to form on the Dragoon from the elbow upward, covering both forearms and fists entirely. The phrasium took the shape of two heavy, spiked gauntlets. It also formed from the knees down, covering the shins.

"Hoh. So she's using her crystal fortification? That's much more up my alley!"

Dominant Constructs could harden their bodies with crystal material. But that was something they could only do to themselves. The ability to harden external objects was a power unique to the Sovereign. Even Phrase like Xeno could make basic crystal structures and use them offensively, but he couldn't freely manipulate phrasium and give it unique shapes or purposes.

Melle was a prodigal genius when it came to the art of crystal manipulation. Ever since he started serving her, Xeno held a tiny ambition within the depths of his heart. His little brother wanted to take the Sovereign's power, but Xeno had no such aspirations. He simply wanted to annihilate the Sovereign, a genius who had managed to unlock the secret of traveling across worlds. He wanted to prove his might to the universe, to show that his martial prowess exceeded her magnificent talents. He wished only to grind her core to dust and let it fade away.

He did not hate her, far from it. Xeno admired Melle. He found her beautiful. She was a supreme being, something far beyond him. That was exactly why he was filled with the burning desire to break her. But the Sovereign vanished from Phrasia one day without any real warning. The sense of grief and loss that Xeno suffered that day was hard to put into words. That's why he was truly thankful to Yula, for giving him the chance to meet the Sovereign again on the battlefield.

Now there was only one obstacle between Xeno and his target. He needed to wipe out this troublesome brat in the machine, so he could have his true battle. Xeno's Fake Gear swung its blade down toward the Dragoon once more. A high-pitched sound rang out as the mech punched the weapon away.

"Mnh?!"

"Now then... Hand-to-hand? This, I like. I'll be using the abilities my master taught me. Better watch out, Xeno."

The Fake Gear's sword hand was suddenly seized by the Dragoon's left. It was dragged forward, allowing Ende to punch the muddy-gold thing in the elbow. A cracking sound ripped upward through the Fake Gear as it lost its right arm.

Even the Fake Gears were weak around the joints. They had to be if they wanted to be as mobile as the Frame Gears they were imitating. But they were still made up of mutated phrasium, so they could regenerate. For regular Fake Gears, they'd just regenerate using the cores of the Skeletons inside, but these ones used the cores of Xeno and the other Dominant Constructs.

The mutants were offshoots of the original Phrase, after all. Dominant Constructs were more than capable stand-ins for basic mutant Skeletons. Though, obviously, the mutants and the regular

Phrase weren't completely compatible. Thus, the regeneration was a little slower than it should have been. And Ende wasn't about to let that opportunity pass him by.

"Combat God: Almighty Palm Strike!"

The Dragoon's palm strike, which was infused with just a bit of divinity, loomed toward the Fake Gear's cockpit.

"Gaugh?!"

Xeno guarded himself with his left hand. It was an instinctive reflex in response to danger, one that had kept him alive several times on the battlefield. The noise of the impact was insanely loud, but Xeno only felt a small impact on his Fake Gear's left arm. However...the arm crumbled away into dust.

"Damn, I missed."

"Wh-What was that power?!"

"That's a secret."

Even though Ende had some control over divinity, he was barely even a beginner in the grand scheme of all things. It wasn't his own power, but more like power he'd borrowed from his master. The God of Combat was a master of controlling chi, and Ende had followed suit in picking up that art as well. He was beginning to make that kind of power his own, just a little.

"I've never been much of a weapon wielder, honestly. I only used the swords with the Dragoon because it's built for that kind of combat style."

If he'd used his hand-to-hand style with the Dragoon in its regular state, its fists would have broken to bits. There was a world of difference between the speed-oriented Dragoon and a Frame Gear like Gerhilde, after all. If he wanted to brawl, he'd have to do considerable remodeling to his Dragoon, and he was actually pretty fond of the Frame Gear as it was. He didn't want to remodel it. But with Melle supporting him, he could bring out his true power. Her crystal could even survive the slight divinity he was leaking.

Ende determined that it would be fine for him to brawl a little recklessly. Though, to be honest, he'd probably only be able to use a divinity-infused attack one more time.

The Fake Gear's right arm regenerated into a jagged blade. Xeno had optimized the regeneration speed by simplifying the limb's shape. The blade arm slashed forward, but it was easily caught by the Dragoon's gauntlet-hands. However...this was exactly what Xeno wanted.

"Get a load of this!"

The Fake Gear's visor released a blinding flash of light.

"Gwuh?!"

The monitor display was bathed in white, causing Ende to lose sight of his enemy. When the light cleared, Ende was greeted by the sight of the Fake Gear thrusting its right arm toward the Dragoon like a spear. It was aiming for the cockpit. Ende took evasive maneuvers, but the muddy-gold blade still sank deep into the Dragoon's shoulder.

"Tsk."

Xeno tried to yank the blade out, but he found himself unable to. He glanced and noticed that Melle's ice-blue crystals had bonded the mutated phrasium to the Dragoon.

"Now, let's try this again. Prepare yourself!"

"Shit—!"

"Combat God: Almighty Palm Strike!"

Another palm strike came forward, this time landing squarely on the Fake Gears' undefended torso. Xeno's Fake Gear finally broke free, falling backward as it crumbled to pieces. The pieces of the Fake Gear rolled along the ground, breaking up into debris until there was nothing left.

"Little bit sneaky to blind me, don't you think?"

Ende wheezed slightly, his borrowed divinity surely expired. His Dragoon was in tatters. He knew that his master was definitely watching the fight...which worried him. He couldn't consider this a proper victory, which meant his master wouldn't view it that way either. That meant there'd definitely be an intensive training course waiting for him a bit later on. The thought of it was unsettling.

But the battle wasn't over. The monitor displayed Xeno's figure, clambering out of the cockpit debris. He was unharmed.

"Sovereign! You who forsook our homeworld! Come out, Sovereign! Come out and grant my wish!"

The red-crystal clusters on Xeno's body began to grow until they coated his entire body like sturdy armor. This was Xeno's special fortification. To Xeno, the fight was far from over. Or rather... the fight hadn't even begun yet. The Dragoon was just the warm-up.

"I will handle this, Endymion. Please watch me from the sidelines."

"Doesn't really feel very chivalrous leaving it to the lady I'm supposed to protect, but...I respect your wishes."

Ende did as he was told, and opened up the cockpit hatch. Melle leaped into the air. She descended gracefully, almost as if she had some kind of control over the fall, and landed just as properly. Ney and Lycee ran to her side.

"Ney, Lycee. You mustn't interfere. It is my duty to finish things myself."

"B-But...Lady Melle!"

"I am the former Sovereign. I cannot turn a blind eye to this. And...if I must be truthful, part of me longs for this battle as well."

Melle smiled softly and began to walk forward. Xeno stood before her, clad in crystal fury. As Melle moved forward, ice-blue crystals began to coat her body. A thin, elegant armor wrapped itself around her shortly after. It was almost like a dress, from the way it flowed. A thin vine of crystal began to curve its way around her as well. The mere sight of her brought to mind the vision of a blue rose personified.

Melle stopped walking. She was the serene blue, facing down a fearsome red.

"No more talk, Sovereign! I'm gonna smash you to bits!"

"If you believe yourself capable. I may have thrown away my status as Sovereign, but that does not mean I discarded my power. I hope you can enjoy what I have to offer...as I tear you limb from limb."

Xeno's grin only widened. Melle's expression remained neutral.

"That's what I'm talking about!" Xeno laughed like a madman, wildly stomping toward his target. He shifted his arms into two crimson blades, intent on slicing Melle apart.

"Prisma Rose."

The thin vine contorted around Melle's body, weaving into a protective net that blocked Xeno's strike. The vines she wielded could serve as offensive and defensive tools. They continued to move, snaking their way up Xeno's blade-arms, then raised his body into the air and slammed him into the ground. His right arm had been snapped off. The vines wrapped themselves around the severed arm, discarding it like simple trash.

"Gahahahaha!"

Xeno clambered to his feet, laughing with renewed vigor. He fired several red projectiles from his left hand. Melle, expressionless as ever, used her vines to strike the projectiles down from the air. But, to her surprise, they exploded on impact with the soil. The ground ruptured, bursting open with Melle right in the midst of it. Dust clouds were kicked up, obscuring the battlefield around her.

A gust of wind blew through, clearing the dust. Melle was still standing, unfazed. Xeno's right arm had regenerated, and he wasted no time reshaping it into a spear. He charged once again at the Sovereign, aiming to impale her in one fell swoop.

"You're mine!"

Xeno felt the tip of his spear sink into Melle's chest, but only for a fraction of a second. She vanished and reappeared behind him in a flash. Her myriad vines seized Xeno and bound him tightly. The thorns along the vines extended, piercing into his red crystalline body. A single vine raised itself high into the air above his head.

"Prisma Guillotine."

The vine grew a sharp blade at the tip and fell downward, cleaving Xeno into two halves. Once again, her vines picked up his bisected pieces and discarded them like trash. When his body was split, Xeno's heart burst with excitement. The fear of being killed by such an overwhelming force as the Sovereign caused ripples of pleasure to run through his body.

"Gahahaha!! This is the good stuff! Battles gotta be like this, or what's the point?! It's gotta be life or death! A desperate struggle against a fearsome enemy, but holding out hope for your own win! This is fantastic! I was born for this!"

"I can't put myself in your position at all, Xeno."

Xeno regenerated his lower body as he pulled himself up by his arms. Melle just stood there and watched him recover. Xeno's body completely regenerated after a few seconds, then started to expand slightly. He was now a touch taller and broader than he had been a minute ago. His features became a little more fierce, almost like he was a crystal beastman. His throat began glowing, exposing the location of his core.

Despite the lack of blood flowing through his nonexistent veins, Xeno's eyes were clearly bloodshot. Ende understood Xeno's rampage as he watched from inside the Dragoon. Xeno had been seeking an appropriate death. Melle understood as well.

"You've decided to don your Zenith Armor? Very well, then. Come at me with all you have."

"GRAAAARGH!" Xeno roared like a wild animal, charging furiously toward the Sovereign. The core in his throat emanated an immense amount of light. Xeno's very lifeforce was being channeled throughout his body. He'd focused everything on this gamble. He was staking every iota of strength inside him on this final shot.

A shrill noise rang out, cementing the destruction. And then… silence. When Ende and the others looked up, they saw Melle standing tall, Xeno's fist caught in her left hand. There wasn't even a single crack of damage running through her crystal body. Melle then began to squeeze, crushing the entirety of Xeno's arm without any change in her demeanor at all.

"I hope this battle brought you satisfaction."

Xeno had no response to Melle's words. The Zenith Armor was a last-ditch effort for the Dominant Constructs. It was an armor coating that shaved away their very lives. After his last attack, Xeno was barely even conscious.

Melle closed her eyes, and a thorny rose stem jutted out from her body. It flicked forward and pierced Xeno's throat. The tiny little core was obliterated in seconds, crumbling to dust. The rest of Xeno's body followed suit, turning to fragments on the ground. The single-minded Phrase, who knew only battle and war, had finally met his match.

Melle turned around, wordless. She didn't bother looking back at the crumbled remains of her former subordinate.

My [Gladius] pierced through several mutant cores, causing them to break down and let out black smoke. There weren't any mutants remaining. A few Skeletons were scuttling around, but Ortlinde Overlord swiftly mopped them up with a couple of stomps.

"Looks like there aren't any more coming..." I said as I turned toward the golden palace. It was oddly quiet. I didn't think that we'd wiped them all out...so I wondered if they were waiting for us to approach.

"Touya, Elze and the others are returning."

In response to Yumina's words, I turned to see Sakura's Rossweisse, Elze's Gerhilde, and Ende's Dragoon coming back our way.

Hm? What happened to Ende? Holy crap, the whole Frame Gear's kind of a mess... I zoomed in my camera on the Dragoon. One of its antenna horns had been snapped off, one leg was missing its wheels, and there was a big hole punched through one of the shoulders.

Welp... Rosetta's gonna have her work cut out for her. Repairing that mess won't be a small feat.

"Looks like you got your ass beat."

"The enemy was stronger than we expected, but we took him out."

I opened up comms and heard Ende reply right away. Seemed like the man himself was completely okay. Elze's voice suddenly interjected.

"We took him out? Don't you mean Melle took him out? I was watching the whole thing. Don't think our master wasn't, either. He's gonna put you through hell later!"

"Touya... Why are your fiancees so..."

"So what? Perfect? I have no idea, they're so great, aren't they?!"

Don't come to me for support against my brides-to-be, you idiot! I'm obviously gonna throw you to the wolves if it comes down to it... I sighed quietly and turned my sights back to the golden palace. Even though we'd been calling it a palace, it was more like a crystal mountain. It certainly wasn't made of gold, just muddied phrasium. It had protrusions here and there, with steep angles jutting outward.

We found something that looked vaguely like an entrance, but it was only four meters tall. Going in with Frame Gears wasn't really an option.

"Let's dismount for now," I ordered as I hopped out of Reginleif and stashed it back in my [**Storage**]. Everyone else did the same, using their rings to store their Frame Gears. Ende put his Dragoon into one of those microscope slides he owned.

We clambered up the cliffside towards the entrance...is what I would've said if I hadn't just used [**Levitation**] and [**Fly**] to bring us all up there.

The entrance was cleanly cut into the side of the crystal mass. It was about four meters tall and two-and-a-half meters wide. The path led straight into the crystal structure, a dull glow emanating from within. Honestly, it smelled way too fishy. There weren't any enemies around at all. The whole thing just felt like a trap. Still, we had to move forward. I decided to set up a couple of contingency methods, just in case.

"[**Prison**]."

I summoned a barrier with myself as the center.

"All right, let's roll. Ende. You watch the rear."

"Gotcha."

We walked down the hallway as a group. It was so silent that we could hear our footsteps ringing out with each push ahead. We didn't know where we'd be attacked from. It created a sense of unease, but we still continued onward.

"Th-This is a long hallway…" Linze timidly muttered as she glanced around. I looked back and noticed that the entrance we'd come through was now so far away that I could barely make it out. The path was on a slanted decline, meaning we were headed downward.

It had gotten darker, so Linze summoned a [**Light Orb**].

"I wonder if they plan to collapse the crystal mass while we are underneath it, I do."

"H-Hey, don't say that!"

Yae's words clearly made Elze uneasy. I reminded them that we'd be unharmed thanks to the [**Prison**] I summoned, and they seemed relieved.

"Mm?" "Oh." "Ah?" Melle, Ende, and I suddenly stopped. Seemed like they'd both felt the sensation I'd just felt.

"What is it?" Lu tilted her head in curiosity. I didn't want to stay silent and intensify anyone's anxiety, so I just explained it right away.

"I felt space kind of like…distort, just now. I think this place is connected to another area of space."

"Another area? Like the hangar?"

"Sort of. It's kind of a pocket space that exists next to your world, but doesn't really exist at all… I believe you guys have been calling this a gap between worlds…" Ende explained the rest. I remembered what God Almighty had told me. That the gap between worlds was a space that connected different worlds across long distances, and it was from there that the Phrase had originally invaded.

"Now then, Touya… How might I explain this to you? Ah… Let me put it in these terms. Do you remember attending school while you were alive? Let us use that as a metaphor. Your individual classrooms would be all the different worlds, and I would be the principal."

"O…kay…"

Huh? What's the old man talking about now? Then again, I guess he does remind me of a certain wizarding world's headmaster.

"Thus, the walls that separate the classrooms from the corridors would be the world boundaries. And…climbing the stairs in the corridors would be like ascending tiers of worlds… Yes, that works nicely. I suppose that would make this place the rooftop? But I digress. Though I have the highest authority in the school, I do not know everything that happens within the school. Each class is independent study and does not always have supervision. Though I suppose if a school did that it would be promptly shut down… But do not think about it too hard, this is just a metaphor."

I could understand what he was getting at. No headmaster could keep track of countless classrooms, especially when some of those classrooms didn't even have teachers assigned to them.

"Now, to continue… Those beings known as the Phrase would be akin to flies or mosquitoes that buzz around the hallways. When the classroom door opens, however briefly, they will try to enter the classroom. Then the people inside the classroom would move to destroy them."

"Yeah, makes sense."

"So the corridors would be the space between worlds. To travel through worlds, you would ordinarily have to go through that space. Only the gods can travel through classrooms without using the corridors. That is the unique ability to travel through dimensions we have."

That explained things. It seemed that each world was connected to the space between worlds. It was this space that the Phrase, and people like Ende, used to hop between worlds. Kind of like how the school troublemakers would always hang out in the hallways.

"It's kind of annoying, huh?"

"Indeed it is. We cannot just indiscriminately spray insecticide in these hallways, either. Doing so would kill the good insects."

I couldn't help but picture the mental image of Ende rolling around on the floor and foaming at the mouth alongside a bunch of dying phrasium lifeforms.

God Almighty was right. Indiscriminate murder wasn't the solution. I sighed quietly as I sipped some tea.

That was how the conversation with God Almighty had gone down. And now we found ourselves in a space much like that gap between worlds.

"They're luring us in here, right?"

"Probably. But we don't have much of a choice but to continue."

We pressed on. Eventually, the corridor ended. We came out into a wide area. The place was too dark to see the high-placed ceiling. The whole area kind of gave off a vibe of some kind of temple... A fitting place for the wicked god.

"Touya... Look at that!"

"Ah...!"

Yumina's voice caused me to look straight ahead. There was an enormous golden mass, kind of like an egg or cocoon, sitting silently before us. It was huge. Far larger than any Frame Gear. It was shaped like an upright egg, with a silky, golden substance reminiscent of spiderweb wrapped all around it. It kind of reminded me of an insect's pupal form.

A lone figure sat atop the stationary mass.

"Yula…" Melle couldn't help but speak his name.

The cold-looking man, adorned in muddy golden crystal, stared down at us with icy eyes.

"It has been some time, Sovereign. I didn't expect to meet you ever again. Ah, and it has been some time since I last saw you as well, Mochizuki Touya."

"Surprised you remember me. You sure look different from last time. Almost like a whole new guy."

His blue crystal body was now a muddy-gold, metallic substance. He'd mutated. His thin, scholarly face had been overtaken by dark gold crystals. This ambitious fool was now completely kin with the wicked god.

"I have discarded my meager existence as a phrasium lifeform. I have claimed this new body, and new abilities. This is an evolution of my base form. Are you not much the same, Mochizuki Touya?"

"Don't group us together, asshole. I'm not the same as you."

I didn't want him to compare himself to me.

"Oh? Well, no matter. You can feel it, can't you? The divinity emanating from the cocoon! Can't you see it? The glimpse of utter perfection from within?!"

Yula's words were true. I'd been feeling a foreboding divinity in our surroundings for a while. I could see that the source was the strange egg-cocoon in front of us. It was a far deeper divinity than what the NEET god had... I wondered just how many negative emotions this thing had feasted on. And so, I raised Brunhild and pointed it right at the egg.

"Sorry to put a damper on your day, but that thing is the wicked god. I'll need to get rid of it. It has no place in the future of our world."

"You pathetic little creatures don't get to decide what is necessary in the new world I'm creating. That honor falls to me."

Yula snapped his fingers, causing a ringing sound to emanate through the area. Several golden pillars rumbled up through the floor before immediately melting down and taking the form of a small skeletal army. Some of the Skeletons were wearing powered suits that resembled the dwarven-made Dverg. They were probably made by reverse engineering Isengard's Gollem technology. I wasn't surprised that we'd been ambushed.

More and more Skeletons rose up from the ground, attacking us with their scimitars. But each of their weapons were deflected with a clang. The [Prison] I'd set around them was an impenetrable defense, after all.

"What an annoying obstacle."

"Wh—?!"

The sound of shattering glass echoed out, and the barrier around us crumbled. Yula had shot out a small laser from his finger, obliterating my [Prison].

Shit. Muddy or not, divinity's still gonna work. The Skeletons won't do much, but I can't reliably defend against Yula... Realizing we were undefended, the golden Skeletons continued their assault.

I dodged an attack, using Brunhild's blade mode to pierce an incoming Skeleton's core. Then, I quickly shifted to gun mode, popping a few shots into some Skeletons behind me.

"Kokonoe Secret Style: Woodpecker Chain!" Yae unleashed several consecutive strikes, shattering core after core without missing once.

Yae, Hilde, Lu, Elze, Ende, Ney, Lycee, and I stared down the Skeletons ahead of us. Yumina, Linze, Sue, Sakura, Leen, and Melle supported us from the back.

"Prisma Rose!" Melle's hands unleashed a flurry of crystal vines, wrapping them around the golden Skeletons in the area. She squeezed them until they were crushed into little pieces. Their cores fell to the ground, where the tips of those vines mercilessly pierced them.

Holy crap. That's terrifying... Sakura sang, supporting us with her magic. Linze used Ice magic to freeze the enemy at their feet. Ende and Elze charged in, punching open their rib cages. Lycee and Ney used their divine weapons to wipe out foe after foe, while Sue and Leen focused on defensive magic to prevent any getting through to us.

"Grugh."

One of the Skeletons in the powered suit came over with a mighty punch. The mechanized, sixty-centimeter-wide fist came flying right at my face.

"**[Power Rise]!**" I roared, fortifying my body with magic, and catching the fist in one hand. I was just about to rip it off, but a bullet from Yumina's Colt Army Model 1860 pierced right through the mech-mutant's core.

Hot damn, that's some fine shooting... The Skeletons definitely weren't enough to defeat us, but it was getting a bit tedious.

My grandpa once told me that the best thing to do when fighting a group was to find a way to take out the boss in as spectacular a fashion as possible. He told me that the wisest way to fight was to just find the guy in charge and punch the hell out of him. I agreed.

"Ende, keep up the work against the Skeletons."

"Huh?"

I didn't waste any time and cast [**Fly**]. Then, I kicked off the ground and bolted toward Yula, morphed Brunhild back to blade mode, and swung it down toward his head.

Yula morphed his arm into a blade and stopped the attack. It was kind of annoying that he'd blocked me so easily. It was even more annoying that Yula flashed a smug grin while he did it.

"I had a feeling you'd attack me."

"Huh, is that right? What, did you prepare something to beat me with?"

I was a bit pissed off at this guy's smug attitude, so I tried sneering back at him.

"Actually, yes."

"Huh?"

Yula smirked again, and several magical barriers triggered with him as the focal point. That wasn't too unusual, since Ende and I often erected magic barriers to defend ourselves. The strange thing about this barrier was…I was inside it as well. I could barely even finish my confused thoughts before I was swallowed up in a flash of light.

"Tou…ya?" Yumina, who was still in the throes of battle, couldn't help but call out in confusion.

Touya had charged up toward that Yula person, but he was suddenly engulfed in a golden explosion…and then he disappeared.

Yumina thought maybe Touya had used teleportation magic, but the effect seemed very different. That mutant, Yula, must have been the cause. He'd successfully removed Touya... The strongest obstacle in his path.

Yumina... No, not just Yumina. All of the fiancees in the room were visibly shaken by what had just transpired. They were his fiancees, but they were also linked to him through his divinity. Through that link, they could feel him wherever he was. No matter how far away Touya was, there was an absolute connection binding them. But right now? That connection had been severed. They couldn't feel his presence anywhere. Touya had been eliminated from their subtle perception, creating a confusingly deep sense of loss within them.

"What just happened to Touya-dono, what happened?!"

"T-Touya?! Touya?!"

"G-Grand duke..."

The girls were quickly plunged into uncertainty. But they couldn't afford to lose their cohesion this deep into enemy territory. Even though Yumina knew that, she couldn't come up with a way to resolve the situation. Their attention was drawn away, resulting in their attacks becoming dulled.

Slowly, the golden Skeletons began to gain the upper hand. Tears welled up in Yumina's eyes as she lost sight of what to do. But suddenly, she heard the sound of a pair of hands clapping together.

《Okay, calm down! Calm down! Hold it right there, you know?》

"H-Huh? Karen?!"

Yumina glanced around in confusion upon hearing the familiar voice, but Karen was nowhere to be seen. Ende and the Phrase girls hadn't heard the voice, either. Only Touya's fiancees had heard it.

《Touya's going to be okay, you know? He got separated from everyone else, but it'll only be for a little while. He'll be back soon, you know?》

Those words eased Yumina's heart. It was true that Karen liked to tease and mess around, but she wouldn't lie about something of this magnitude. If she said Touya would be coming back, then it had to be true. Yumina believed in Karen whole-heartedly. Everyone had their confidence restored by her words, leading them to take the advantage over the Skeletons again.

《It's a little dangerous over there right now, you know? I think you should make a break for it.》

"Huh?"

Just as Yumina was about to question what Karen meant, the ground began to rumble and shake.

"An earthquake? But how?"

"Gh... The space is breaking down!" Ende grumbled as he smashed another Skeleton.

"We need to get out of here. This whole pocket dimension is about to collapse. If we're still in here it'll crush us with it. Melle, can you take us out of here?"

"I can. But what about Touya?"

"He won't be beaten by something this small. I'm sure he'll be back before we know it," Ende proclaimed. He did not doubt that Touya would be okay. Touya was a dependent of the god of worlds, a being far above his incredible master. Ende knew that Touya wouldn't die even if he was killed. It was basically a waste of time to worry about his odds of survival.

Melle spread out her crystal vines on the ground by Ende's side. They formed a wide circle.

"Everyone! Get in the circle!"

CHAPTER III: WARPED ASPIRATIONS

The girls all entered the circle, bashing a few Skeletons on their way. Ende hopped into the circle last, and the circle spread out, producing more vines that pierced through several Skeletons.

Melle took that opportunity to trigger her dimensional transfer ability, taking the entire group with her. But...within the rumbling, collapsing dimension, another sound rang out. The sound of a shell splitting open.

"...So, where are we?"

I glanced around, realizing that I'd been pulled somewhere. I couldn't see anything of interest in my surroundings. The place wasn't dark or anything. It was just empty. The whole area had a sunset-orange hue, and some misty clouds of dull gold blew by here and there. It was like the spirit realm, but completely different. I couldn't feel any spiritual energy here.

"I'd like to welcome you to Niflheim, my divine-suppression realm."

Yula stood in front of me, bowing politely. This bastard really pissed me off. He had the gall to welcome me here when he'd dragged me by force.

"...Huh?"

I was unable to properly visualize my destination.

"It took a great many resources and a great amount of time to construct. This realm is not connected to any other world; it's completely isolated. Even with the power of a god, it would take a great deal to escape this place. The only drawback is that this place only functions so long as I am within it..." Yula's words rang clear.

This place was designed to isolate me, so it was designed to make it near-impossible to escape. He'd brought me here with himself to trap me.

I tried using my divinity to warp away, but it was hopeless. It was like I'd been thrown into Aokigahara on the side of Mt. Fuji without a compass or a map. I had no idea where to go. It was basically impossible for me to anchor on to any landmarks. If I could focus my divinity it'd probably be easier, but it was being interfered with somehow.

"It's pretty impressive that you managed to create something like this. But if I defeat you, it'll vanish, right?"

I morphed Brunhild to gun mode and pointed it at Yula. He just smiled.

"That would be most unwise. The world would indeed collapse upon my death, but it would collapse in on you. You wouldn't be freed."

"Gh…"

I had a feeling that was the case. That was probably why he'd brought me in. He didn't necessarily want to defeat me. He just wanted to immobilize me. The only thing I could reasonably do was slowly try to find a world to pinpoint on to with my divinity, and try and warp to it.

"Well, it's true you may be able to return eventually. But I can't say the world will be in the same state you left it in."

"What do you mean?"

Yula grinned as projected images began appearing in the air around us. I could see a live feed through each of them, of Brunhild, Belfast, Regulus, Strain, Allent, and various others. Just about every country was visible. But why was he showing me all that?

"Don't you think there were too few of us defending the crystal fortress? It's true that we may not be able to choose where we appear from the breaches between worlds… But, with a little bit of focus, we can certainly choose when to emerge."

"Wait, don't tell me…!"

Yula smiled wide as I caught on to what he meant. Behind him, in the skies of those kingdoms…cracks began appearing everywhere.

"M-Miss Relisha! We've got spatial errors all over the world! These readings are off the scale!"

"Gah!"

The first organization to notice the impending threat was the guild. Their sensors picked up on the disturbances, with every single one in the world picking up on them at once. The emergence points all had identical estimated arrival times. No matter how many times Relisha tried to call the grand duke, her phone calls wouldn't connect.

One of these cracks had appeared right by Brunhild, though Relisha felt like their Frame Gears could probably win out. That wasn't the case for the other nations, though. It was true they knew when the enemies would emerge, and how many there were… But most countries in the world didn't have Frame Gears. The ones fighting the mutants would be the knights, soldiers, and whatever adventurers were available. Relisha knew that it would lead to a massive loss of life.

The mutants, on top of killing people, transformed their prey into their own kind. This was an incoming crisis on a global scale, and there was nothing Relisha could do. She let out a horrified gasp as she gripped her smartphone, the enormity of the situation washing over her.

"Grand Duke… Is it not ready yet?!"

Relisha was hoping they'd be able to pull through with the trump card that Touya had mentioned, but it was looking hopeless.

"Please... Please... Hurry!" Relisha could do nothing but quietly pray as her subordinates started calling out emergence locations.

■　■　■　■　■　■　■　■　■　■

"Your Highness, you must flee!"

"Nonsense. A king must not flee and leave his people to their fate."

The king of Belfast calmly sat atop his throne. He scowled at the cowering nobles. Their fear was understandable, however. The spatial disruption had appeared right next to Belfast's capital. There were around five thousand mutants expected to pour out of it. If they all attacked the capital at once, then it would surely fall.

Most of the nobles wanted to leave, but the wise king knew it would be wrong to leave before evacuation procedures had completed.

"Viscount Swordrick, has our knight order finished strengthening our defenses?"

"Yes, sir! Our men have taken up positions outside our walls! We've enlisted the local adventurers as well!" Viscount Swordrick, wearing his Eashenese armor, said as he bowed to the king. The Eashenese katana on his waist rattled as he moved. Swordrick, the greatest swordsman in Belfast, prepared to move to the front lines.

"We must fight hard, for the sake of those struggling in Isengard right now. I entrust our protection to you."

"Yes, sir!"

As the king spoke, his smartphone began vibrating. He glanced at the display.

"Mismede's beastking, huh...? Ah, hello?"

"Hey, King Belfast. How're things over there?"

"Not great. They're about to emerge near the capital. It's very stressful..."

"Wahahaa! Same here! I sent all our best men out to intercept, but it's gonna be a rough fight for sure."

The beastking's voice was positively jolly despite the grave nature of their conversation. But he was a man who craved battle, so he was probably looking forward to the great war ahead. But the king of Belfast knew that wasn't the only reason for his relaxed attitude.

"It's not here yet, is it?"

"Pfft, nah. You know how Touya likes to take it easy. But frankly, I hope it comes soon. If it doesn't, we'll be in a whole heap of trouble."

They were relaxed because of that young man's special trump card. They were sure it would come in time, so they were just holding out until they could use it.

The two kings watched their retainers hustle and bustle in a panic, calmly waiting to be saved.

■　■　■　■　■　■　■　■　■　■

"Send our war priests and our templars at once! This is a holy war, I say! A divine test from god above! We must protect our loved ones by mustering all our strength! May the blessings of the divine be upon you, my child!"

"Yes, ma'am!"

The captain of the war priests, along with the commander of the templar knights, hurried out of the pope's chambers.

Fortunately for the Ramissh Theocracy, the spatial disruption had appeared far from the capital city. Unfortunately, it was still near a few smaller towns. The guilds had been helping coordinate evacuation efforts, but the situation was not all that promising.

The pope clutched her smartphone to her chest, silently praying. She prayed, not only to the almighty god that she believed in, but also to the young man who she believed to be his messenger.

"Your Holiness."

"Phyllis…"

The pope raised her head and saw Phyllis, clad in a well-fitted cardinal robe. She was the right hand of the theocracy and the only other person who'd seen God Almighty alongside the pope. She gripped her smartphone as well.

"Do you think it'll come in time?"

"I do, yes. The light of salvation will come to us before long."

"I feel the same. The grand duke and his fellows must be facing the brunt in Isengard right now. We must do our part as well. I trust in you, Phyllis."

"Thank you, ma'am. I promise I'll stake my very life for the sake of this world."

The two of them clutched their smartphones, awaiting deliverance.

■　■　■　■　■　■　■　■　■　■

"Looks like something big is going down…" Sarutobi Homura heaved a sigh as she looked down at the news app on her smartphone.

"Mutants all over the world… Are things going to be okay?" Fuma Nagi looked up from her own phone. They were currently stationed in a guard building in Brunhild.

"We will be fine. The grand duke already saw this coming, and the guilds have been preparing squads to help defend," the calmest of the three Brunhild ninjas, Kirigakure Shizuku, spoke matter-of-factly. She was also holding her smartphone.

"Do you think that thing the grand duke mentioned is gonna get passed out soon?"

"Probably. No other way we can survive this."

"I'm looking forward to it, honestly... But it's a little scary too..."

"Steel yourselves, girls. You are warriors of Brunhild. Act like it."

The sudden voice, coming from nowhere made the trio yell out in shock. It was Tsubaki, the leader of the intel corps. They hadn't sensed her arriving at all, prompting them to jump in surprise. Tsubaki quietly sighed, making a mental note to intensify their training.

"You know what you have to do, don't you?"

"Y-Y-Yes, we do! As soon as the download comes up, we'll head out!"

"Good. Stay in constant communication, and act as one. No matter what happens, don't get cocky. Got that, Homura?"

"Whaaat?! How come you only singled me out?!"

Tsubaki took out her smartphone and gripped it tight. She couldn't help but be nervous. The plan was absolutely absurd, after all. Only the grand duke of Brunhild could have come up with such brazen insanity.

■　■　■　■　■　■　■　■　■　■

"Doctor. Would it not indeed be better to distribute it before the mutants emerge?"

"We need to hold on as long as we can. It'll be more effective with more magical power fueling it," Doctor Babylon quelled Liora's fears as she flourished her lab coat like a cape.

They were surveying the spatial disruptions on the research laboratory's monitors. The monitors displayed direct feeds from dozens of tiny wasp-like drone Gollems created thanks to Elluka's expertise.

"Seventy-eight emergence points globally... Indeed, they're almost in every nation. If this goes unchecked, it'll be a repeat of what happened five thousand years ago!"

"And that's why we're going to make sure that doesn't happen. Tica, how's the mana gauge looking?"

"Combined with the amount, mmh...that master spurted inside? We're allocating resources from the Tower as well. We have enough to supply them all."

"Good... Very good!" Doctor Babylon nodded proudly in response to Tica's words. She'd been left in charge of distributing a particular app. She'd explained it to Liora earlier, but the timing was vital for an important trump card like this. It needed to be unleashed at the right moment.

"When our opponent thinks they've won, that's the pivotal moment... We'll charge in and wreck them, and cause them major trauma at the same time. Not that those mutants will get it. It should piss off that Yula guy though," Doctor Babylon grinned as she said that, pulled out an ether vape from her coat pocket, and puffed on it for a few moments before exhaling a cloud of smoke.

"He might think he has the upper hand on Touya, but we're ready for it. This is my revenge, five thousand years in the making! We're gonna get real weird with it!"

Doctor Babylon had previously learned from Ney that Yula was the one responsible for the grand invasion during the ancient era. She wasn't exactly the patriotic type, since she didn't view her homeland as anything more than the place she grew up in. However, it was also home to some people that she liked quite well.

She wouldn't say it out loud, but the opportunity to avenge those souls had finally come. She'd be a fool not to take it.

"Doctor. The disruption in western Regulus has opened up, mutants inbound."

"Spatial tear in northern Strain has indeed opened as well. Mutants all over, indeed they are."

"We don't want them to cause major issues, so it's time we did it. Operation Full Moon is a go. Begin the distribution!"

"Indeed! Launching the app!"

And just like that, Liora brought her fingers dancing along her work station, sending it out to all those who possessed a smartphone.

Mutants tore through the fabric of reality, pouring in all at once. Brunhild, Belfast, Regulus… They all emerged at the same time, starting their advance. I couldn't see any Upper Constructs. Even if there were, they'd have been too big to break through as quickly as the other ones.

"Heh… Heheh… Hahahaha! Now my kin will assimilate all living creatures of your world into our species. I will stand at the apex of a new, mutated species! I will use that power to continue crossing through worlds until even the gods are within my grasp!"

Yula seemed positively elated as he watched the live feeds of the mutants marching on the nations. This guy's goal was to assimilate other species into his mutant army and eventually march on the divine realm. Was he a complete and utter idiot?

I sighed quietly as I watched the mutant forces march on the displays behind him.

"What is it? Are you speechless? Feel free to lament your own lack of power all you like. Even with the power of a god, you're still an insignificant little human. A pathetic dog such as you could—"

"You know, the world I come from has a lot of stories..." I suddenly cut Yula off and started talking. I didn't need to listen to his prattling anymore. After all, the app distribution was probably about to begin.

"So these stories have lots of different kinds of protagonists, and it goes without saying that there's a ton of different antagonists as well. The antagonists can usually be sorted into different categories based on the patterns of their behavior. You know, like... This kinda bad guy is gonna do this thing, or this kinda bad guy is gonna do that thing. Basically, bad guys can be pretty easily stereotyped."

"...Where are you going with this?"

"Well, here's the thing. Antagonists like you are the type to take hostages. I feel like you'd have probably gone after those close to me or those I considered friends. I knew you'd target the people of the world I'm trying to protect. That's why I set a certain measure in place."

This wasn't a very heroic line of thinking, but it was smart to aim for your enemy's weak points. I did that all the time, honestly. But that was why I knew a snide, calculating enemy like Yula would want to as well, so I had something in place to oppose him. And it had just arrived, right in the nick of time.

"Hm? And? Am I supposed to believe there's something you can do from here?"

"Oh, I won't be doing anything, Yula. Everyone else will fight in my place. Sure, I may be trapped here, but they're in another world. With their smartphones."

I held up my phone, pointing out the newly added app to Yula. I'd left it to Doctor Babylon, but I wished that she'd picked a cooler icon for it...

Beneath the icon, which was a cutesy version of my face, there was a simple, two-word name for the app.

Mochizuki Touya.

"It's finally here!"

The beastking looked at his phone, cheering loudly once he saw the app appear. Most of his nobles looked at him in confusion, but Royal Chancellor Glatz and a few others who also had smartphones inexplicably started cheering and flexing.

The beastking began downloading the app as soon as he could, but he could barely contain his excitement. Once it downloaded, he anxiously brought his trembling finger to the app icon. And, in a flash, he felt power unlike anything he'd ever felt before flowing through his veins.

"Oooh! It's incredible!"

He rushed out to the castle courtyard and began focusing his power. He'd always wanted to do this.

"**[Fly]!**" the beastking screamed right before he soared upward into the air.

"Oh! I'm flying! I'm actually flying! Ahahaha!"

He looked to his side, and Chancellor Glatz was also flying. The beastking thought this was a bit redundant, since Glatz was a winged beastman. He just assumed that the guy wanted to try it out, much like he did.

"**[Storage]!**"

The beastking pulled a sword out from nowhere. It was huge and crafted from phrasium. This version of **[Storage]** was shared between all users of the app. Weapons, armor, and even food had been stocked inside it well in advance. Whoever took what was automatically recorded, and if anything was broken or lost, then they'd be able to pay for it later.

"Glatz! I'm headed out!"

"Huh? Your Beastliness?!"

The beastking soared off to the south. Once he activated his beloved [**Accel**], he started rocketing through the air.

"Amazing! I'm already at the battlefield!"

The royal soldiers stood at the southern plain, ready to face down the incoming mutants. They were outnumbered two to one. And so, the beastking stopped in mid-air and decided to use [**Speaker**] to rally his men.

"Warriors of Mismede! Show no fear this day! Give those shimmering schmucks something to really think about! Show them our might! I'll be fighting by your side, so battle with all you have!"

The Mismede soldiers cheered and waved their weapons in the air. The beastking grinned wide, pointing down his hands at his men.

"Come forth, Winds... Blessed be the Updraft: [Tailwind]! Come forth, Light... Blessed be the Flesh: [Skin Barrier]!"

The beastking enchanted his entire army with Wind magic to enhance their speed and Light magic to enhance their defenses. The battle would go a lot easier as a result.

"Warriors of Mismede, charge!"

"HRAAAAAAAARGH!"

Thus, the true battle began.

"Hyaaah!"

The man swung his spear hard, slicing a mutant in half like it was made of butter. Phrasium weapons were amazingly durable; he hadn't chipped his spear at all.

The emperor of Regulus loved being wable to fight again. His old bones no longer creaked and his body was instead filled with vigor and might. And in order to test out the magic, he tried something he'd been wanting to try for a while.

"**[Slip]**!"

The mutants that were headed toward him tumbled in a straight line, allowing the Regulus knights in their Chevaliers to take them out easily. Thankfully, there had been enough basic Frame Gears in the shared **[Storage]** for all the nations to have some.

"Your Majesty! Please, fall back! It's too dangerous!"

"Don't be foolish, my friends! I cannot fall back now, not at all! Touya would surely laugh if I quit in the thick of it!"

The emperor of Regulus simply laughed in the face of his concerned knights. Then, he pierced the core of another mutant that was shaped like an ant and watched as it melted away.

The emperor had fought many battles during his youth. The fire inside him had dimmed during his old age, but this battle was reigniting the spark once more.

"How very exciting! I feel just as vigorous as I used to be!"

The emperor gleefully swung his spear around like a child playing with a toy. He destroyed mutant after mutant with ease. He wasn't in a Frame Gear, yet he fought just as skillfully as the men in the Chevaliers. This was, in part, due to his thorough experience as a young man.

"Come, my knights! Follow me! Let us rid our fair land of these wrongdoers!"

"Hoo-rah!! All hail the emperor!"

The dull-golden glow of the mutants was gradually purged from Regulus.

"Meow, meow, and meoooooow!" Mr. Mittens screeched as he unleashed a sword flurry, piercing through various mutant cores until he finally felled the last one in the area. He'd beaten a whole batch by himself.

"Meow then...where to next?"

Mr. Mittens sheathed his crystal rapier as he turned to his fellow warrior, Athos. Athos, who looked like an American shorthair, checked the map on the smartphone-on-a-string he had dangling from his neck. He skillfully swiped along the phone with the soft toe beans on his paw pads.

"East Roadmare. Small village called Cattenip. Around ten mutants."

"Sounds like a tasty village..." Porthos, the tubby Persian cat, peeked at the map and made a small comment.

"Ten rascally mutants? Let us march off to save the day, gents!"

The elegant Siamese cat, Aramis, raised his sword skyward. The other cats drew their swords and met his.

"All for one, and one for all!"

"Well then, let's get those meowtants! [Teleport]!"

Using Sakura's Null spell, Mr. Mittens and the others warped off to save the day.

Piercing claws shredded the mutants, and hulking bodies crushed their cores.

Shirogane, the draconic butler of Drakliff Island, was leading an army of Dragons against mutants that had appeared in the Gem Kingdom.

"Don't leave a trace behind! Our master, Touya, has ordered it!"

"Ping." "Pong." "Pang."

Shirogane, still in the physical form of a silver-haired young man, cast out his arm as he ordered the attack. The three maid Gollems, Ruby, Saph, and Emerl, imitated his pose.

"Graaargh!"

Giants of all shapes and sizes faced down the mutant horde. Though the mutants absorbed the fire breath, the White Dragons capable of breathing frost managed to slow down the enemy advance. The rest of the Dragons took that chance to charge at the foes, their attacks strengthened by Shirogane's support spells.

One of the mutants began charging up a particle beam blast toward Shirogane...

"[Shield]."

Only to be effortlessly blocked by the man's magic. That spell could block just about anything, save for an Upper Construct's beam attack.

"My, this magic is certainly splendid. I'd expect no less from Touya," Shirogane said as he smiled and gripped his smartphone, praising his employer. He was overjoyed that he could muster such strength in a humanoid body.

Touya's enemies were, naturally, his enemies as well. Shirogane would not let a single golden insect escape his wrath.

"Purge them all! Don't let a single one escape!"

"Ping." "Pong." "Pang."

"Heh... They're really going for it. It's pretty cool watching them go wild."

"Wh-What nonsense is this?! How can those mere creatures be mustering this strength?! What did you do, you bastard?!"

I grinned a bit, seeing Yula's cool demeanor break apart. The look on his face was fraught with anger, confusion, and fear.

"Just a little power I like to call nunya."

"And just what the hell is nunya?!"

"Nunya business."

I laughed obnoxiously, taking great joy in taunting Yula. He snarled at me, fire burning in his eyes. He clearly didn't think the situation was all that funny. I was pretty amused that he could make that kind of expression, but maybe the cool facade had been an act from the beginning.

The tide of battle was turning thanks to the Mochizuki Touya app. As its name implied, it was an app that allowed people to do what I could do. They'd have access to every single magical attribute possible, and their physical prowess would be multiplied severalfold. Obviously, divinity stuff wasn't accessible, though.

They could use as many spells as they wanted too, since the app tapped into a deep mana well within Babylon that I'd been regularly topping up. This was my ultimate trump card. It was only to be deployed in a situation where I'd be unable to help them, so they'd be able to help themselves through my power. It was a means to entrust those I believed in to save the world themselves. It was honestly a little reckless, so I wanted to save it as a last resort. But back at the summit we'd had earlier, the world leaders did say they'd be happy to defend the world with their own hands, so I trusted them. Plus, the fact that the app download had reached my phone meant that I had a bridge to the other world. Though there was a little bit of a signal delay, apparently.

I grinned, holding out my arms and starting a call on my phone.

"Y'ello. Yep, I'm good. Actually, I'm glad you waited, since it let me realize I could make an outgoing call. Yeah, good call on your part."

"…H-Hold on. Who are you talking to?"

"Hm? Oh, yeah. I got pulled into some weird dimension. Don't worry about it, I'm fine. I can trace my way home now."

"Wait, is that a communications device?! That's impossible! How could it be functioning?!"

"Sorry, Doc, gimme a sec… Yo, Yula. Dude. Can you shut up? I'm on a call right now. Hold on, I'll call back, Doc."

I abruptly ended my call with Babylon. I could understand Yula's frustrations. This realm was supposed to be his, after all. Nothing was supposed to be able to come in or out without his say-so, not even stuff like light or sound. Given that I was here, in his personal space, making an outgoing call to someone he'd never met before… It was pretty clear why he'd be upset.

The mass-produced smartphones were a product of Babylon, but mine was different. It was a legitimate sacred treasure, something imbued with the divinity of God Almighty. Back when the Reverse World was still separated from the regular one, getting service was a pain. That was solved when we had a dimensional disruptor constructed to link both worlds, but now the world was merged it was basically irrelevant. Since I didn't want that kind of trouble to happen again, I'd asked God Almighty, who'd been in the mortal world at the time, to help me out with cell reception. He happily lent his aid, saying he figured it'd be useful for me to have phone contact when I eventually went back to Earth for a little while. It didn't take him long at all…

That was why I wasn't too worried after being brought to Yula's dimension. Frankly, I just wanted to avoid having to call Karen and asking her to come pick me up... That would've been way too embarrassing. Still, now that I'd had enough time to get my bearings and pinpoint my relative location via my phone, I could freely leave.

Ordinarily, I'd have taken care of the moron in front of me, but I didn't want to risk the space around me collapsing. I'd have probably been able to survive if I triggered a full Apotheosis, but I didn't want to run that kind of gamble.

"Ney told me about you. She said you were a strategic genius, but you rarely dirtied your own hands. You've never come to the front and stared your enemies down, have you?"

"And what of it? So long as I have pawns that can be easily manipulated, why should I do the legwork?"

"That's why you're a fool, Yula. You think too little of your enemies. I think the fact that you got a hold of a little bit of divinity went to your head."

"Stay your tongue! You've a lot of nerve, when you're exactly the same!" Yula snarled furiously at me. He seemed to think that we were similar in that regard.

"Dude... Do you even know how weak that wicked god is? I mean, like...do you even know what kind of god was used to create it?"

"Of course I know! The god himself told me of his power! He was an unfathomably powerful god, above any other! He was the unbreakable god of order! He called himself a neat god, for some reason, but I'm sure he was just being modest... Wh-Why are you laughing?!"

I couldn't help but burst out laughing at Yula.

Pffftahaha! You idiot! He wasn't a neat god, he was a NEET god! Oh man, okay... Okay... Calm down, Touya. I can't believe this. This is amazing... That idiotic, pathetic NEET god must have given him an easily misunderstood explanation. Kind of like someone ashamed of being unemployed explaining things in an easily misconstrued manner. Like saying you work private security without specifying that you stay in and watch your own house all day.

I remembered the Dragon king guy who tried to forcibly control Dragons with that needle artifact to help him take over the world. He was pathetic, and apparently, Yula was just as bad. Guys like him lied, tricked, and manipulated to get whatever they wanted. They ended up using those stronger than them to reach their own ends. They refused to dirty their own hands, saw themselves as higher than the people they toyed with. They all decided of their own volition that their enemies were lower than trash, and devised plans to sweep them away like they didn't mean a thing. That was why they always got what was coming to them.

In Yula's eyes, he probably thought everyone except me and my immediate family were worthless small fries. He probably thought they wouldn't be worth worrying about. That was his fatal, arrogant mistake.

"Look, you at least deserve to know this. That god you found? He was the lowest ranking divine being around. He was what's known as a servile god. Actually, his rank was even lower than that because he got kicked out of the divine realm for abandoning what little duties he had."

"Excuse me?!"

To be honest, the wicked god was probably a lot stronger now, given it had eaten up so many souls. The fight against it was going to be a pain in the ass. There were a hell of a lot of golden Skeletons among the mutant armies, so it must have consumed at least that many human souls. Still, I had no obligation to add that on to what I was saying.

"Either way, Yula. Whatever you were working toward ends today. You can sit here and watch me take it away from you."

"Bastard...!"

I pictured the coordinates from my phone in my mind and locked on to my world. Then, I warped away. Yula tried to say something, but it was too late. I was gone.

"Whoa! C-Crap! [Fly]!"

I was a little bit shocked to find I'd come out in the middle of the air. I'd found myself hurtling down from hundreds of meters in the sky, which was scary! It was a bit hard to fine-tune my destination using a long-distance warp like that, after all. I looked down just to be sure I was actually back in the right world. And when I did, I noticed a city with a huge tower in it, which I vaguely recognized to be Isenberg.

"Looks like I'm home safe... Now, what about the others?"

I landed atop the tower and pulled up my map. My fiancees were safe and sound, a short distance from Isenberg. Seemed like they'd escaped the golden palace, and I knew they had the Touya app as well. Everything was okay.

"Wh—?!"

Right when I was starting to relax, a sudden chill ran up my spine. I immediately recognized the aura washing over me.

"No way..."

I turned to look at the golden palace and found that it had been replaced by an immense pillar of light. The light swayed like heat dancing in the air. I could tell at a single glance that it was unfettered divinity. It wasn't a pure divinity, like that of Karen or God Almighty.

It was a disgusting, twisted divinity. It was steeped in muddy-gold darkness, like an amalgamation of negative human emotion.

The hazy divinity shot upward until it took form in the air.

I couldn't even think of a proper way to describe it succinctly. Its upper body was insect-like. It kind of reminded me of a silkmoth. It had massive compound eyes, antennae on its head, six insectoid arms that jutted out from its sides, and moth-like wings on its back. Its lower body was long, kind of like a snake's stomach. Its belly swelled softly, emanating dark divinity from inside.

So far, one of the largest things I'd gone up against was the witch-king's massive Gollem. But this thing? It was several times larger. The beastly form it originally had was completely gone.

It slowly flapped its wings, descending to the golden palace below. When it landed, it crushed the muddy-gold structure to tiny fragments. I wondered if those wings were just for show, since they hardly seemed suited for giving its massive body full flight.

There it stood, atop the wrecked mass, almost asserting its dominance over the landscape.

"…So it finally hatched, huh? The wicked god's matured form is on full display."

Those grim, shimmering compound eyes swiveled around and glared right at me. It knew exactly where I was.

Skreeeeeeeeeeckh…

The wicked god flapped its wings, emanating a noise that resembled nails on a chalkboard.

Glimmering powder sprinkled from its wings, scattering across the land. It was probably the same spore-stuff that the golden tree from Isengard was releasing a while back. It transformed people who died while harboring negative emotions or people who were just especially wretched.

It wasn't effective against people like me and my fiancees, but if I left it be, then the spores would probably spread all around the world.

"Reginleif!"

I summoned my Frame Gear and leaped from Isenberg's tower. Then, I used [**Fly**] to soar into the cockpit, setting my smartphone beside the monitor and firing the machine up.

The display showed the wicked god turning toward me.

I heard a whirring sound, and particles of light began forming between its antennae.

Oh shit!

"Gah!"

I took emergency evasive maneuvers, swooping down low and getting far away from the tower.

Around three seconds later, a huge ball of light crashed into the tower, creating an explosion larger than any I'd ever seen before. The wind pressure created by the blast came rushing toward my Frame Gear.

"[**Prison**]!"

I secured Reginleif in a barrier, preventing chunks of rubble and metal debris from hitting me.

A mushroom cloud rose up from the impact site, black smoke trailing off it like a volcanic eruption. Suddenly, hunks of rock began falling from the sky.

I rose higher up as the barrier kept on getting pelted by the falling stone. Then, I looked down to survey the situation.

It was even worse than I'd feared. The city of Isenberg had been completely wiped off the map.

The city had already been forsaken because of the golden Skeletons, but now there wasn't even a trace of it left. The blast had carved it out of the earth.

That attack was far, far beyond the might of an Upper Construct's particle beam. If it had been a lively city filled with people, that would've been utterly catastrophic...

I had a feeling I wouldn't be able to block that attack with [Prison] or [Shield], and [Reflection] was probably a no-go too...

"No point sitting around on my ass. I better try attacking."

I split off the crystal boards on Reginleif's back and merged them into a large blade.

"Gonna need a greatsword for this..."

The massive sword, which was honestly more like a gigantic triangle, pulsed as I channeled divinity through it. Phrasium was a great conductor for mana, but it also happened to channel divinity really well.

I raised my newly forged holy blade and sent Reginleif charging toward the wicked god. The six limbs that jutted from the monster's torso fired out laser beams, as if they'd been waiting for my move.

I weaved in and out, deftly dodging the incoming blasts. Then, I closed in, swinging my blade hard and severing one of its thin limbs. Thin was a relative term here, since, due to the sheer size of the wicked god's body, even one of those arms was wider than Reginleif. Despite the phrasium blade's divinity and strengthened composition, I met a surprising amount of resistance while cutting through.

The severed limb dropped to the ground and smashed to pieces. *Creaaaaaaaaaaaak...*

The wicked god's entire body sounded like it was moaning as it regenerated the missing limb. I'd expected it to have that kind of ability, but I'd needed to be sure.

"Blaze, o Fire! Blazing Penetration: [Burning Lance]!"

A massive, flaming lance appeared in the air and flew toward one of the wicked god's wings. The magic attack pierced right through the wing, leaving a scorched hole. Still, the wicked god was so large that it was akin to burning a hole through a piece of paper with a cigarette. It regenerated the damage in mere moments.

"It didn't absorb the spell... Guess it didn't retain that trait from the Phrase, then?"

The Phrase lifeforms were capable of absorbing magic and using it to strengthen themselves. But it seemed the wicked god didn't have that ability... Or maybe it just didn't need it.

It could use its divinity to instigate its own regeneration and could fire lasers without an external magic source.

"This thing's real big. I really don't know how I'm gonna kill it..."

If it was a regular organism, it would die if I went for the head or the heart, but then I kind of wondered if gods could even die... No, if the divine venom could supposedly kill gods, then it would be possible to kill this imperfect one.

I started thinking too deeply, failing to notice another laser barrage.

"Aw crap!"

I grabbed the controls and just barely evaded the strikes... Or at least, that was how it should have gone. But the wicked god flapped its wings, causing an air current that knocked Reginleif off course!

Before I even had time to react, a laser hit my Frame Gear directly, blasting it back.

"Guh..."

IN ANOTHER WORLD WITH MY SMARTPHONE

"Protective Barrier Damaged. Operating at sixty-five-percent efficiency."

A voice came from my smartphone. The protective barrier around Reginleif prevented the mech from taking direct damage, but it seemed like it'd only be able to take around two more direct hits before breaking.

I righted Reginleif's position and glared down at the wicked god. I didn't think it felt anything like emotion, it was probably just attacking me on instinct.

The wicked god had basically been formed from the negative emotions of tens of thousands of people. It was just a mass of hatred, now. There wasn't a dominant personality controlling it.

Even that NEET god had just fallen into the mass of darkness, alongside the rest. Not that I was too surprised. NEETs weren't exactly known for their strong wills.

The wicked god suddenly bellowed, as if enraged by something, and launched several laser blasts at me. It couldn't have read my mind, could it? Those lasers were really dangerous, so I needed to focus.

This kind of battle was like facing a boss monster on a blind run. I didn't know its attack patterns. I had no idea what it was weak to, either. And so, I had no choice but to be conservative.

Man, this really does feel like a boss fight. I can even hear the final boss music from a certain famous JRPG series in my head... Hold on a sec... Huh? That's not coming from inside my head! Why's the final boss music from a certain famous JRPG series coming out of my cockpit's internal speakers?!

I turned to Reginleif to try and identify the source.

"What?!"

The display on the monitor showed a man sitting down in mid-air. He was furiously strumming a guitar, which was hooked up to some speakers from Babylon's storehouse. It was Sousuke, the god of music.

"Ohhh, hic! Wowshers."

"It's pretty impressive, you know? Wicked gods like this don't show up all that often."

Suika, the god of alcohol, was standing nearby with a bottle in her hands. Karen, the god of love, was also there. She was eating some potato chips.

They were just sort of sitting there, marveling at the wicked god.

"H-How come you guys are here?!"

"We're, hic, on a trip! The god of agriculture went to the, hic, puretree. Then the three fighty ones are busy fighting the, hic! The uhhh… gold thingiesh, and now we're here!" Suika giggled a bit as she spoke. This scene didn't exactly fit the mood… I was supposed to be engaging in an epic clash for the sake of the world! They were treating it like a picnic!

"I just came to see if you were doing well, you know? I guess you'd call this an employee evaluation?"

"Whatever it is, it's goddamn annoying!"

C'mon, guys! I'm trying to fight here! Let me have my moment!

"Don't worry about it, hic! We got told not to interfhere… We can give ya plenty advische, though."

I stared at the little drunkard, wondering what kind of advice a gremlin like her was supposed to provide. But suddenly, Sousuke's guitar tune changed.

I turned back toward the wicked god, just in time to see its massive, snake-like tail barreling toward us.

All three of the nearby gods teleported away, which felt pretty unfair!

"Gah… [**Teleport**]!"

I copied the others and warped away to safety.

The massive tail crashed into the ground, splitting it apart. If that had hit Reginleif, I definitely would've been flattened like a pancake.

"How am I even meant to hurt that thing?"

"Wicked gods are formed when a source of divinity merges with a source of grudge or negativity, you know? They're monstrous apparitions that are imbued with the power of the divine. So only divinity is gonna work!" Karen popped up nearby and spoke plainly.

"Uhh… Haven't I been using divinity this whole time, though?"

"You've been usin', hic! Ushin' divinity but alsho not divinity. You got too much, hic, attacshment to this world. You're all mixshed up, Touya! You're, hic, like a cocktail! Cocktails are way niiice, but, hic, pure distilled is better! Get it?! You gotta be a spirit, Touya!"

"… Karen, what is she saying?"

I didn't understand what the hell the little drunk was trying to say. I didn't know why she was calling me a cocktail, or what she meant by attachments.

"Well, it's kind of like this, you know? You're a mix of godhood and humanity right now. You're using divinity, but it's still impure because of your attachment to your humanity, so it can't show its full power, you know? But at the same time, you can't become a full god either, or else you won't be allowed to interfere with this world's issues. You need to channel pure divinity through your body and make use of it…all while keeping your human body intact."

"And, uh…how do I go about doing that, exactly?"

"You need to affirm your own goals, Touya. You need to gather your determination to defeat the wicked god, and to leave behind any lingering doubts about your godhood."

Karen's explanation kind of made sense. Or well, the whole attachment part did, at least.

It was true that part of me just wanted to keep on living my regular human life. Obviously, I wouldn't become a full god right away, but I was still afraid of setting myself down a path I wouldn't be able to come back from.

But I had to come to terms with the fact that I was already on that path. I hadn't gone down it very far, but I'd definitely been walking it for a while. Despite that, I was still worried about leaving my humanity behind… So at least in that regard, Suika was right about me having lingering attachments.

I even knew that a tiny part of me would be okay losing to the wicked god if it meant I didn't have to fully embrace the divinity inside me... But I couldn't do that, since it would be a slap in the face to all the precious allies that brought me here.

"Hurry up! Right now, you're lingering too hard on something pointless, like a guy who got dumped and won't stop thinking about his ex. You aren't a stalker, are you?"

"What's with all the weird-ass metaphors?! Ugh... Whatever, I kinda get what you mean. Thanks, Karen."

"Heheh, of course," Karen said as she grinned and flashed me a wink, Sousuke strummed at his guitar.

...Why did you just strum a level-up sound effect from a video game? How am I supposed to interpret that?!

"Heeey, hic! Don't thank herrr. I gave you the advice! Spirits! Distilled spirit, that's what you gotta be!"

I still couldn't understand that annoying little gremlin.

I sighed slightly as another barrage of lasers came flying in at us. Karen and the others warped away, just like before.

"Do your best, you know?" Karen's voice rang out before she faded into thin air. The three of them had clearly opted to watch this battle from a safer distance. To gods like them, this was somewhat of a casual day out, like going to a baseball game.

"All right... Better not disappoint my crowd, then."

I began to swirl divinity around my body. Suika's comment about me being a cocktail kind of made sense. My magic power, something tied to me as a human, was always mixed in when I used it. I had to distinctly separate the two things.

I decided to use God Almighty as a reference point. My divinity came from him, so it shared the same characteristics as his own. All I had to do was replicate the pure divinity that he emanated during the Ramissh incident. I needed to distill my own divinity, to create that kind of aura. Despite the intensity of this task, I felt oddly calm.

A strange light drifted up past my mind's eye, staying in the center of my focus. At first, it felt like a tiny little spark, but at the same time, I could feel it expand like a grand explosion. It was the spark of creation within me, something new being born.

I opened my eyes and felt a strange rush of power through my body. It was divinity running through me. But it wasn't like before, when I'd garbed myself in it. This time, it was flowing out from within.

I'd done it. It was a strange feeling, but it was kind of like assembling a plastic model and the parts just slotting perfectly into place after a little push.

It happened so seamlessly that I was amazed that I'd never managed it before. I knew in my heart that this divinity was my own…and that it would be okay for me to embrace it.

The power I exuded spilled out into Reginleif's ether liquid, spreading across the entire Frame Gear. Naturally, the phrasium greatsword in Reginleif's hand was also filled with pure divinity.

Karen's divinity had a kind of pink tinge to it, and Moroha's felt like a sky-blue with a little gold lining. But my divinity? My true divinity? It shone with a silver…no, a platinum hue.

It was different from God Almighty's divinity. This color belonged to me.

Another laser barrage came in from the wicked god. I dodged it and slashed at the wicked god's limbs just like earlier. This time it was different, there wasn't as much resistance in the cut. It was like chopping through a potato with a kitchen knife.

Creaaaaaaaaaaaaaaaaaaak!

The area I'd cut began to go up in black smoke, and the wicked god's body began contorting in agony. I'd just severed a limb, but it wasn't growing back. It fell to the ground and melted into viscous sludge.

I did it... That means I can win this!

"Touya, are you all right?!"

I suddenly heard Yumina's voice over the comms system. I turned around and saw the girls in their Valkyries. They were headed in my direction from the ruins of what had been Isenberg.

But...just as I saw them, I also saw particles of light gathering between the wicked god's antennae. It was charging up its attack much faster than the last time too. I barely even had time to process what was happening before it launched the same attack that had obliterated the city right toward my fiancees.

I was about to activate [**Teleport**] in order to save the girls, but I stopped when I noticed a surge of magic in their vicinity.

The strike impacted, leaving an enormous crater. This one was even bigger than the first. If the girls had been in the impact zone, then not a trace of them would have remained.

Thankfully, that wasn't the case. All the girls were on the ground beneath Reginleif, perfectly safe in their Frame Gears.

The moment they saw the orb of light headed in their direction, they activated [**Teleport**] themselves and moved right to me.

They hadn't done it via Sakura's power, even though it was her spell. The Mochizuki Touya app was still active, so they simply borrowed my power and did it that way.

"I'm glad you're okay, Touya."

"Yeah. Sorry, you guys. Yula sealed me away for a while there. I managed to bust out, though."

Man, I must have really had them shook. Wait, hold on a sec...

"Where's Ende and his group?"

I looked around but I could only see my nine fiancees. Ende, Melle, Ney, and Lycee weren't in the area.

"We had Melle and the others go help fight the mutants. The Dragoon was pretty banged up, and we didn't really wanna make them fight against this thing with just their bodies," Elze answered over the comms. That was fair. Even with the Mochizuki Touya app, going bare-fisted against the wicked god probably wasn't the wisest idea.

"So that is the wicked god, it is..."

"I like the size, but I don't like the bug parts!"

Yae and Sue offered their comments as everyone looked over the enemy. Its enormous compound eyes focused on us. I couldn't sense any emotion or will coming from it at all, it was just a being of pure instinctive chaos.

Particles of light began sparking between its antennae. An attack was coming!

"Everyone, fan out!"

On my command, the girls used [Fly] to soar upward with their Frame Gears. And right after we moved, a bolt of lightning flew from the wicked god's antennae and scorched the ground where we'd just stood.

Its attacks were just as big as its body. It was kind of a pain, honestly.

"Touya... Um, I wanted to ask something..."

"Hm? What is it?"

"This power that's flowing through us... Is it yours?"

"Huh?"

Linze's words were a little confusing, so I glanced a little more closely at her and the girls. They had platinum divinity emanating from their Frame Gears.

What the...? That's just like mine! Are they receiving it because of their connection to me? Wait, this also explains how they were able to move their Frame Gears with [Fly] and [Teleport] too.

My divinity had improved the breadth of their skills.

"This certainly feels warm."

"It's like the grand duke is right by me... I know we can't lose..."

"Heheh. We're all wrapped in our darling's love."

"We got Touya's love on our side, now! We're unbeatable!"

Ugh, that's embarrassing! I-I know it's true, but don't just say it out loud!

"All right, girls! Let's take Touya's love and use it to strike down our foe!"

All the girls nodded in unison, moved by Yumina's words. Then, they began emitting their own divinity from within their bodies. It wasn't as strong as mine, but it was every bit as pure.

The realization hit me like a truck. The girls had already made up their minds to walk with me on the path of godhood. They hadn't hesitated in the slightest. They had no lingering attachments. And that meant I'd been the most indecisive person here. I felt a little bit of shame.

"Let's do this!" Elze spearheaded the charge, nimbly weaving in between the laser rays.

"Take this! My chi-infused finisher! Cannon Break!" Gerhilde smashed a pile bunker into one of the wicked god's limbs. The massive arm wasn't broken off, but cracks spread across the entirety of its surface. And those cracks then began to smolder and smoke. Elze's divinity was preventing it from regenerating.

"Hiyaaaah!"

"Haaaaagh!"

Next came two Frame Gears, one purple and one orange, Yae's Schwertleite and Hilde's Siegrune. They each swerved toward the cracked limb, raising their blades high.

"Kokonoe Secret Style: Dragonfang Disaster!"

"Lestian Sacred Sword: Sixth Roaring Thunder!"

Their two slashes intersected, creating a mighty cross against the enemy's arm. The limb shattered like a glass sculpture, breaking to pieces and tumbling to the ground.

Black smoke continued to rise from the wounds in its body. The wicked god responded by launching a barrage of lightning toward the three Frame Gears that had just attacked it. But they managed to avoid the attack by simply teleporting away.

The wicked god started scanning the area with its compound eyes, but suddenly, a bullet enchanted with [**Mega Explosion**] smashed into one of those eyes.

Skreeeekch!

The wicked god found itself jostled by the impact. Another bullet struck it in the throat, detonating on impact. The explosion left a few trails of fire on the surface of the wicked god's body.

"It's an easy target, that's for sure," Yumina spoke up as Brunnhilde hefted its rifle and launched a third bullet. This one struck the enemy's belly, erupting into another massive explosion.

Another explosion rang out on the monstrous being's shoulder. But that one hadn't been caused by Brunnhilde, it was thanks to Lu's Waltraute. The emerald mech had used its C-Unit attachment to launch a bombardment.

"Wow, it really is easy to hit! My aim isn't so good, usually!"

Shiiiiiiiiiiiiiiiiiiiieeeeeeeekch!

A strange noise rang out from the wicked god as it raised and fluttered its wings. The strange sound carried an unusual force with it, rocking our Frame Gears with a shockwave. The sound it was emitting had muddied divinity imbued into it. Our Frame Gears were being crushed by an intangible force, somewhat similar to the effects of **[Gravity]**.

It was probably a way to prevent us from getting closer, but we had something to counteract that.

"That won't work..." Sakura's Rossweisse blared her muttering from its speakers, and then Sakura broke into song. She was singing the same song she'd performed during the battle against the mutant Upper Constructs. It was a pretty straightforward song about the power of love that was associated with a popular time travel movie. "That's the power that makes the world go 'round" and all that.

The wicked god couldn't stand in the way of such a force. Its attack vanished thanks to Sakura's song, and we could move again.

"Now it's my turn!"

Sue's gigantic golden Frame Gear, the Ortlinde Overlord, pulled a certain weapon out of **[Storage]**. It was the specialized anti-Upper Construct giga gravity weapon, the Gold Hammer. It was an enormous golden ball covered in spikes.

Ortlinde Overlord clutched the handle and tugged on the long chain before starting to spin in a massive circle. She began with a horizontal spin before pulling it in closer and spinning it vertically. The magi-graviton particles began to accumulate within the throwing hammer's main body thanks to the effects of **[Gravity]** and **[Prison]**.

Schhhhkkkrreeeeeeckh!

The wicked god shrieked, raining lasers down on Ortlinde Overlord. The mech seemed utterly defenseless at a glance, but Sue had the power of the Mochizuki Touya app on her side.

"[Reflection]!"

A translucent barrier appeared in the air, deflecting all the laser blasts far off into the sky. Then, the Gold Hammer began sparking, prompting Sue to finally let go.

"Crumble to dust!"

The golden ball, now a swirling mass of magi-graviton energy, soared toward its mark. The wicked god, likely sensing the danger, swung its tail up to deflect the projectile.

The moment the weapon made contact with the tail, we were assaulted by a blinding flash of light that filled up the entire sky.

Schhhhkkkrreeeehh?!

Half of the wicked god's tail evaporated, turning to golden dust and flying away with the wind. The Gold Hammer broke down with it.

"Aw, I messed it up."

If this were an ordinary set of circumstances, Ortlinde would've been broken down due to the Gold Hammer's recoil, but we'd made several tweaks to the mech's design since then, and the extra magic from the Mochizuki Touya app meant that it was still functional.

"I wish I had another Gold Hammer, but I'm all out!"

"You did well, but you can leave the rest to us!"

Sue's lamentations were met by Leen's voice. I looked back down toward the ground.

Leen's Grimgerde and Linze's Helmwige were prepping a gigantic cannon. It was the Brionac, our specialized magic artillery. The ultimate weapon prepared for deployment against Upper

Constructs. It required a crazy amount of precise magical control, as well as a deep well of mana, to fire out its massive drill bullet.

It was just a bit too hard to control alone, and the Leen and Linze combo only allowed for one shot. It was pretty unwieldy.

That wasn't even getting into how long it took to charge it up... But apparently, the two girls had accounted for that, since they'd been charging the weapon up since the fight started. I could tell because the meter was almost completely full.

"We're ready to fire!"

"Launch it!"

A massive explosion rang out, propelling the drill bit toward its target. The drill hit the wicked god's belly, starting to rotate at high speeds. It began shredding the creature, digging deeper and deeper with each rotation.

Skreeeeekch?!

The wicked got let out a piercing scream, powerlessly glaring down at the drill bit.

The drill bit continued piercing through the wicked god until it fully penetrated and burst out the other side. If we looked at this on human terms, it would be like someone having a golf ball driven through their stomach. That would pretty much be lethal, but the wicked god didn't have internal organs or anything. That being said, the monster was definitely injured by the divinity-infused bullet.

Skreeeeeeeeekkkkcccccccchhhh... Ghh... Ghho... Ghhhoood...

"Huh?"

The wicked god suddenly stopped moving, and it started making noises in a voice that I recognized.

"I am a God... I am absolute... I am sublime... I will not forgive those who dare defy my right... You filthy, scuttling insects... Perish underfoot!"

Light began to glow from the wicked god's body. A rainbow-like haze appeared in the air around it, and cracks started running all over its surface. Then, beams started bursting out of the wicked god's body as its entire back split open. Its silkmoth-esque wings fell to the ground with a great crash, along with some of its outer shell.

Something started emerging from the hole in its back. Rainbow-colored particles of light, kind of like the colors you'd see on the back of a CD or DVD, flowed out and took the form of leathery, bat-like wings.

There were three pairs, forming six in total. Though they were shaped like bat wings, there was something strangely artificial about their structure.

A jagged back rose out from the hole, following the wings. After that, six limbs pulled out as well, shedding the old body like a discarded husk. These arms weren't insectoid like the shell's, they were large and muscular. The area between the elbow and the forearm was coated in a black exoskeleton. Equally beefy legs burst forth from the lower body, and a new, thorn-lined tail exploded from the halved stump of the old one.

The newly emerged head resembled an iron helmet, with menacing horns jutting from either side.

The insectoid shell fell apart as the creature within finished shedding it, revealing its full presence to us.

The divinity it emanated was a far cry from the muddy gold I'd been feeling. It was releasing a pure, rainbow-colored light. But its body didn't really seem organic at all. Its structure wasn't something that felt like a natural occurrence.

It was almost like... Or rather, it was completely like a mechanical structure. This rainbow-colored wicked god had the distinct form of a twisted, warped Frame Gear.

It was somewhat similar to the witch-king's Gollem, but that one was more clunky-looking. This one clearly had remnants of its Phrase origins in the design, but it was sleeker. If the Hecatoncheir was a mere robot, then this was more of an android. It gave off that kind of vibe.

It felt like it was trying to imitate life, but the uncanny valley was still right there. It felt wrong.

"Foolish, puny mortals... Pathetic little humans who only exist to consume, waste, and corrupt the land they walk... Pathetic... Pathetic... You misguided fools! You should have just obeyed me from the start!"

There was no doubt as to the origin of the voice. Annoying as it was, it was someone I hoped had died.

"...Long time no see, NEET God."

"...Mh? You wretch! You foiled me last time, didn't you?! This is all your fault!"

"Don't blame me for your screw-ups, pal. You reap what you sow."

"Silence!"

The tips of the horns on his helmet began glowing before firing off a triple-barrage of laser fire in my direction.

"[Shield]!"

I didn't want to use **[Reflection]** for fear of the lasers hitting anyone else, so I simply blocked the attack.

The wicked god stepped forward, white smoke billowing from its body. The long, spiky tail slithered behind it.

"You pathetic little interlopers! I would have created a perfect world if you had only let me! Free of war! Free of poverty! Of discrimination and injustice! Why would you deny me?! All I wanted was a truly equal world, governed by justice and pure order!

The beings of this world are lesser than the divine, so there's no harm in showing them the light! It's a god's job to guide and lead lesser beings, is it not?! We could have lived in a true society, a society where I was the unquestionable ruler!"

I didn't really have a response for the word vomit he'd just spewed at me. Judging from his infantile behavior, God Almighty had made the right call when it came to not promoting this jackass. Maybe he'd thought the guy would learn and grow as a person over time, but there was no saving him now. He thought his ideology was absolute and just wanted to impose his way of living on others.

I quietly willed my next command, and Reginleif's greatsword morphed into forty-eight daggers that circled my Frame Gear like satellites. Each of the daggers emanated platinum divinity, almost looking like they were on fire. I wasn't about to show the foul creature any mercy. He was an enemy of my world.

"[Gladius]"

All forty-eight platinum-imbued projectiles flew outward, piercing the neo wicked god's arms, legs, wings, chest, and head. They all stabbed at the enemy full-force.

When the attack finished, they returned to their standby position, orbiting my mech as the neo wicked god recoiled in pain.

"Gaaaauuugh! You little shit! You little brat! You're just a human playing dress up! I am the real deal! I am a real god! I cannot forgive you, do you understand?! You are a lesser being! You're pathetic, something cobbled together in the corner without any true power!"

"Enough. Let me tell you something, buddy. See, back home, there are all kinds of political structures. But we have a word for what you wanted to create. It's called a dystopia."

Reginleif's daggers blazed with platinum fire once more, ready to put an end to their mark. I was ready to put him down, to destroy this selfish, egotistical maniac. He'd gone on rambling too far, and this world was sick of hearing him talk.

"**[Gladius]!**"

My platinum blades ripped through the air, intent on slicing the wicked god to ribbons.

"You miscreants! Miserable ants! You dare to look down upon me?! Me?! I am a god! A being who has lived eons! I will now pass down my judgment upon you!"

Even as my **[Gladius]** strikes pierced his body, the neo wicked god continued to berate us. He waved his arms and summoned lightning from the sky. Each bolt was extremely powerful, and the slower Frame Gears of the group, namely Grimgerde and Ortlinde, couldn't avoid any of them.

"You two okay?!"

"I'm good! Barrier wall is down by forty percent, though!"

"Same here. We can probably only take one more direct hit like that."

The barriers around Reginleif and the Valkyrie Gears automatically blocked incoming damage, but it wasn't an absolute defense. An extremely powerful strike would be enough to break it, and it would eventually wear down after a few strong strikes as well.

The barriers had been created with a considerable amount of magical power, which was a testament to just how powerful those attacks were. And they were also way too quick to avoid with **[Teleport]**. Sakura would probably have managed, but the others weren't experienced enough to get away in time.

"You won't get away, worms! Get a load of this!"

The wicked god's six arms flexed, and he fired laser blasts from his fingers. We suddenly found ourselves under fire from thirty-six bolts of light.

"Gah!" "Eek!" "Mh!" Hilde, Linze, and Yae took direct hits. Their barriers weren't broken, but they ended up being knocked back by the sheer force. With their balance lost, it left them open for another attack!

"Stardust Shell!" Sue's Ortlinde Overlord suddenly charged forward, reaching out its left hand as it emanated a starry light. The light transformed into a protective shield that coated the other girls.

When the lasers stopped coming, Ortlinde Overlord held out its right arm and pointed it at the enemy.

"Cannon Knuckle Spiral!"

The mech's arm detached at the elbow and launched forward, smashing into the neo wicked god's throat with a glorious rocket punch. A little bit of the wicked god's skin was bruised in the process.

"How about that, huh?!"

"You vermin! I could understand if it was that scumbag… But you're mere humans! How dare you attack me! I am a god, I am above all! How dare you damage my opulent form! I will never forgive you!"

The neo wicked god roared, emanating rainbow-hued divinity as lightning crashed all around us.

"You're not a god anymore. Not a real one. You're just a wicked imitation. Hell, I'd hesitate to even call you a demi-god."

"SILENCE!"

The neo wicked god held up his arms and spread out his hands. His palms began to glow different colors. One was red, one blue, one green, one brown, one yellow, and one black. I had a sinking feeling about what those colors represented.

"He's calling down elemental magic! Look out!" Leen warned everyone, beating me to the punch. In an instant, we came under assault by a raging inferno, a frigid blizzard, a roaring tornado, a barrage of rock, a lightning-imbued laser, and a hideous black smoke that seemed to writhe as it traveled.

The laser came in first, forcing us into evasive maneuvers. We managed to use [Shield] and [Reflection] to block the fire, ice, wind, and rockfall. Then, we used [Teleport] to move away from the incoming black smoke. I could tell it was some kind of curse-based magic, probably similar to [Energy Drain].

The laser we'd dodged obliterated a nearby mountain, while the deflected inferno scorched the earth below, and the blizzard chilled the air around us.

It was absolute environmental destruction. The neo wicked god was certainly equipped to wreak havoc upon the world.

"I am a god! You hear me?! An immortal, a divine being! I am the rightful ruler of this world, I am the rightful god of this world! Kneel before me! Take your natural positions...and beg for your lives!"

"I'm really getting sick of this... You're not a god anymore. Not a real one. We're sure as hell not kneeling before you, either. You're just a deluded idiot, prattling on about stuff he doesn't have any business involving himself in!"

Talking to him was clearly pointless, since he was too far gone to listen to reason. Part of me felt a bit sorry for him.

He refused to accept that things were going downhill for him. He was stuck in the belief that he was right, and everyone else was wrong. It was pathetic escapism. He was just lashing out and blaming others for his own insecurities.

I was amazed that someone who'd lived so long as a servile god was really capable of kicking up such a noisy tantrum. From where I was standing, it seemed like he'd just wasted away his entire life.

"You're pretty pathetic, aren't you?"

"Enough out of you! You are a fool, I am in charge here! I am a god, beyond petty human squabbles!"

"...Buddy, look at yourself. You're lashing out with a whole bunch of negative human emotions, aren't you? You're angry, you're jealous, you're clearly upset. You're in full-blown hysterics right now. You're not above anything, you're acting like a human. A child, at that."

"Me? Acting as a human?! Don't make me laugh, worm!"

His tail suddenly arched upward, launching several spiny barbs into the air. The barbs blew up once airborne, revealing a cluster of smaller spikes that were set to rain down below.

It was the same type of attack as the cluster bombs used by Upper Constructs.

"[Prison]!"

I summoned a barrier around myself. If my power hadn't fully awakened, then the attack would have definitely broken my defenses. Luckily, my platinum divinity kept me safe.

The girls managed to use defensive magic to protect themselves too. But then, all of a sudden, the wicked god swung his arms upward. The falling spikes detonated, releasing a fine golden mist that washed over everyone except me, since I was still in the **[Prison]**.

"Oh no!"

"Wh-What is this?!"

"Nghn... M-My strength is...fading, it is..."

The golden mist swirled around, prompting the girls to lose their balance in the air. They all went crashing to the ground.

I started to feel a strange sense of nausea as well...before I finally realized what had happened.

"Gwahahahah! I hope it hurts, vermin! That's all the divine venom I've been storing within my body! Now, I'll grant a slow and painful death to those women, and after that, I'll finally move on to you... Don't think you can—"

"Shut your mouth. Now."

Divine venom? Killing Yumina and the girls? Does this childish bastard really think I'm gonna let him come here, throw a tantrum, and hurt the people I care about?! What the hell is this guy's problem, huh? He's absolutely goddamn hopeless. I'm putting him down for good.

"You better shut the hell up now, you pathetic NEET fuckhead. You're the one always blaming others for your mistakes. You're the one who trashed everything just because he was insecure!"

"Wretch! You still talk ill of me?! I'll—"

My platinum-hued divinity began surging and bubbling within me until it finally boiled over. My blood began pumping in overdrive, unfettered divinity surging through my veins until every pore in my body exuded the pure, platinum sheen of my godhood. Any dizziness and nausea I'd previously felt was gone.

"Wh-What kind of power is that?!"

I glared down at the pathetic imitation god and called back the forty-eight daggers. Then, I morphed them together until they took the form of a greatsword.

Not big enough. I need a bigger weapon to destroy this piece of shit... Almost as if responding to my thoughts, my divinity began gathering around the blade, giving it a larger form. The divinity wrapped around my blade hardened up...until I was wielding a shining, platinum holy blade. I knew instinctively that this blade was designed to smite the wicked.

Did I just use my divinity to…create something? This feels weird…
I used that power like it was second nature to me…

"Wh-What?! Impossible! H-How did you Treasurecraft so easily?! Th-That's a power only the upper echelons of the divine have!"

"Enough. You don't belong in this world."

Reginleif easily hefted up the holy blade. I charged forward at unprecedented speeds and immediately used the weapon to cleave off one of the neo wicked god's arms.

"Aaaaauuuugh!! Wh-What?! H-How did you hurt me?!"

The severed arm burned away to ashes mid-fall. But I didn't stop there. Instead, I swooped down, swinging my blade once more. And that time, I lopped off the tail. My blade cleaved through the entirety of the appendage like a knife through butter.

"AAAAAARGGGH!   Y-You   bastard!   You   insect! E-Enough of this!"

"You're still spouting stuff like that? Aren't you meant to be some sublime, all-powerful god? Or did you mean you were the god of crying and pissing your pants?"

"I'LL KILL YOUUU!"

The failure god lumbered forward in an attempt to grab Reginleif, but I nimbly avoided all of its swipes. I even sliced off a few fingers in the process.

"GRAAAAARGH!! DAMN IT! DAMN YOU TO HELL! WHY IS THIS HAPPENING?! I'VE WORKED FOR THE GODS FOR THOUSANDS UPON THOUSANDS UPON THOUSANDS OF YEARS, AND THIS IS WHAT I GET?! I CAN'T HAVE JUST ONE TINY WORLD AS MY REWARD? ARE THE GODS SO STINGY THAT I CAN'T EVEN HAVE ONE LITTLE WIN IN MY LONG, MISERABLE LIFE?!"

"This world might be little to you, but it's my home. The fact that you'll never understand what it means to its people is why you'll always be a failure."

He just saw the world as a reward, something to be claimed. He didn't care about the people living on it. He just saw them as cannon fodder or ants. Who would want to be in the care of a god like that?

God Almighty and the others didn't interfere in the mortal realms much, and that was because they believed in freedom for all the people below. Even if the worlds struggled sometimes, or hit strange dead ends, they believed in the people and their ability to work things out long-term.

That was why they were real gods and not this pathetic imitation. He couldn't ever understand the feelings or connections between people. Someone like him could never be truly divine.

I wasn't quite at the level of becoming a real god, but I knew I would never become someone like him. I would work hard, for the sake of everyone who put their faith in me.

"[Copy]."

I let go of the beautiful holy blade in Reginleif's hands, which then split off into an identical copy of itself. The two blades then became four, which became eight, constantly dividing until there were a total of forty-eight holy blades circling Reginleif.

I'd never heard of a Null spell called [Copy] before. I just knew that it was an ability I could use, somehow. It could've been part of the Treasurecrafting ability mentioned by my enemy, but I didn't have time to think about it.

Reginleif's arm pointed into the sky, and all forty-eight swords turned their blades toward the neo wicked god.

"Y-You bastard, no! What are you planning?! Stop! Stop! Stop, stop, please! Stop! Don't. Don't you dare! Nooo! I don't want to die!"

"And I don't care. [Claiomh Solais]."

The forty-eight greatswords streaked through the air like missiles, leaving a platinum trail in their wake. I heard the sounds of metal piercing flesh, and saw the blades enter his shoulders, chest, arms, legs, belly, and head.

"GRAAAAUUUUUGH!"

The failure before me screamed out in agony as his body began to split apart. The holy blades gouged and writhed in his wounds, increasing the damage.

The wicked god arched his spine, falling back due to the pain. And the holy blades, still embedded inside him, almost looked like grave markers as they pointed up from his body.

"I'm a...god... Sublime, and...all-powerful..."

One of the holy blades split back into twelve crystal boards before flying back to Reginleif's back. The other holy blades faded away like mist.

The once-mighty body of the wicked god began to flake apart, dissolving into rainbow-colored sand. The sand broke down into even finer grains until eventually, it vanished into black smoke.

I glanced over to the girls, still fallen in their Valkyrie Gears. I reached out my hand.

"[Delete]."

The golden powder was washed away in an instant, wiping out the divine venom from the world entirely.

"Are you girls ok?"

"Ugh... I feel a little weak, but I should be all right... I'm sorry, Touya... You had to do most of the work in the end."

"That's okay, Yumina. I think, in the end, it had to be me handling it, anyway."

Brunnhilde rose up from the ground, followed by all the others. Thankfully, none of them were badly hurt.

"Now then, let's wrap this up."

I reached out to my smartphone on Reginleif's console and began contacting the other leaders around the world.

"Th-This can't be! How did that mortal defeat my god?! Just what is he?!" Yula stood within the Niflheim boundary, totally dumbfounded by the events he'd just witnessed.

This was an utter nightmare. He'd been aiming for the power of a god, and then he wished to seize a world of his own. But now his ambitions of controlling this world and one day returning to dominate Phrasia had gone up in smoke.

Just what had he done wrong? Just where had he miscalculated? He'd fed the cocoon with all the souls it required. He'd done everything to the letter.

Was Mochizuki Touya telling the truth? That this god he'd staked all his faith in was actually a weakling...? Could he really have gotten so carried away with elation that he'd overlooked the fact that he'd been lied to? This just wasn't fair. How could he have been so stupid? Yula, filled with rage at this turn of events, slammed his fist into the wall of his barrier world.

But something began happening when he looked at his fist. Something that utterly horrified him.

"Wh-What?!"

The color was draining from his body. Yula's muddy-gold form had lost its divine blessing, and as such, was reverting to a dull lead-like color.

Niflheim, the entire realm around him, also began breaking down. This was only natural, of course. It took the power of a god to create and maintain a world, even a small one like this, and now that power was gone.

The live feed from around the world showed the mutants losing their color as well.

"N-No! My plans! H-How can this be?! Gah... F-Fine, plan B, then! I'll return to Phrasia and make the young Sovereign my puppet, and then I'll..."

"I don't think so."

"What now?!" Yula roared as he turned around and saw something that made a chill run up his spine. It was his former leader. Standing by her side were the two Dominant Constructs he'd traveled alongside in the past, and a young-looking white-haired man who wore a white scarf.

"Sovereign?! H-How did you come here?"

"A friend from another world told me where I might find you."

Melle waved her smartphone lightly. Ende was familiar with the method of traveling through worlds, and now that Niflheim was breaking down, it was just a matter of looking for him.

"Gah!"

"Prisma Rose."

Melle cast vines from her right hand, snaring Yula in them and slamming him to the ground.

"Gaugh!"

"You've been awfully persistent so far, Yula. But it's time to pay the piper."

Melle's words were devoid of feeling. Yula knew how frightening the Sovereign could be, and now that the ice-cold rage was directed toward him, he was terrified.

"It was my error in failing to recognize your greed, Yula. I didn't want to believe that such wickedness would be in my immediate vicinity... It was my own naive nature that caused untold destruction across countless worlds. Touya dealt with the brunt of it, but it's time I put an end to this for good."

As her right hand continued producing vines that stretched out and trapped Yula, Melle suddenly raised her left. A thick, crystal vine extended from her left hand, forming into a long blade at the tip.

Yula started to muster all the power he could in an attempt to summon his Zenith Armor, but his lead-grey body didn't shift. He had lost the divinity within him, along with the phrasium characteristics he was born with. It was at this point that the reality of the situation sank in. Yula was about to die a truly meaningless death.

"W-Wait, Sovereign! Please, have mercy! A-At least grant me an honorable death on Phrasia. A-At least grant me that, please! Honor our traditions!"

"There's no honor in this, Yula. Begging just makes it worse, so keep quiet. Accept your fate, and break apart. At least there's quiet beauty in that."

"W-Wait! No! Stop! Stop! I can't die here! I'm not meant to—"

"Prisma Guillotine."

The blade came swinging down, slicing cleanly through Yula's neck, and obliterating the core before he could finish his sentence.

Yula's body crumbled to pieces before it began dissolving into a black haze.

"N-No, why... I... I'm..."

Yula had brought countless worlds to the brink of darkness. He had led armies of Phrase on a mindless campaign of slaughter. But in the end, in a dark space between worlds, Yula pitifully died. And eventually, nobody would remember his name.

Even after we beat the wicked god, the mutants still remained in the world. Even when the wicked god's divinity left their bodies, weakening them and turning their bodies a dull grey, they still survived.

The mutants had been freed from Yula and the wicked god, but their directive to kill humans was still something that ran deep. Thus, they continued trying to do exactly that.

But they'd lost their abilities to regenerate, and they'd also lost their ability to harden their bodies. They were about as powerful as generic Stone Golems. The mutants, now weakened, were easily dispatched by knights and adventurers around the world.

We also decided to fly around the world and pick off any we found, which was kind of tedious work, honestly. Still, someone had to clean up.

There were many countries where mutants appeared all over the place, but some nations didn't have any emergence events at all. Some locations suffered major losses and damages to their towns, while others didn't lose a single building.

The world had been saved, but I wouldn't forget the losses we'd incurred that day. Thinking I could save the day without anything going wrong was sheer arrogance on my part.

All in all, it took about two more days to completely wipe the mutants from the face of our planet. And with everything settled,

Brunhild put out a formal announcement to the other countries. Thus, tentatively, the world came to know peace.

After everything was dealt with, I went back to Brunhild and fell asleep. I was out so hard I didn't even dream.

"Mmh...?"

I woke up in my bed, but it was still dark out. I glanced at my smartphone, noticing it was only five in the morning.

The Mochizuki Touya app had been removed from everyone's phones. It was the pivotal piece that led to our victory all around the world, but it squeezed Babylon dry of almost all its mana stores. Everyone kind of went hog wild with it, but we wouldn't have won so quickly otherwise.

"Hmnh..." I yawned and stretched my arms before throwing on a coat and heading out to the balcony.

The sun was just starting to rise. I could see faint traces of light around me.

I sat down at the table and reached into [Storage] to produce a pot of coffee and a mug. Then, I poured out the coffee and took a sip. It was good.

"Would you mind if I partook in a drink?"

"Of course I wouldn't."

I took out another mug and placed it in front of God Almighty, who appeared before me as if out of nowhere. I set down a little cup of milk and a sugar bowl for him as well.

"I see you are no longer caught by surprise, hm?"

"Well, I'm kind of used to it now. But it might be because I fully awakened to my divinity."

"I would say it is likely because it is me. You and I are connected by divinity, my boy. I have a feeling that if it were Karen, you may have been a bit more surprised."

Dang. And here I'd thought that I'd just gotten used to their random popping-up.

"I suppose congratulations are in order, are they not? You have vanquished the wicked god, and purged the threat from this world. I, through my authority as the god of worlds, do hereby acknowledge you as my kin. Though your divinity is certainly enough to match gods of the highest echelon, your formal position would be just above the servile gods."

"Starting from the bottom, huh?"

"Alas, that is how it must be. I cannot show favoritism solely on the basis of us being connected through divinity. That being said, the other gods are aware of your potential and our connection. I am quite certain you will be fast-tracked to a high status. It should only take around ten-thousand years."

"That's hardly fast-tracking to me..."

"Now, now... After the first two or three thousand have elapsed, ten will feel like a mere blink of the eye."

That reminded me of something the French philosopher Paul Janet once proposed. It was a law about psychological time in relation to the self.

The idea that when you were a little kid, a whole day could feel like forever. But when you were an adult, a whole year could pass without you realizing.

At fifty, a year was a fiftieth of your entire life, but at five, it was a whole fifth. Janet proposed that this proportional length affected how we perceived time.

Basically, when you were a kid, everything was new and unique, so those new experiences felt longer and fresher. But as you grew and repeated the same processes, your brain optimized the handling of those things and made time seem shorter. Still, putting that on the scale of thousands of years felt wild.

"So, what'll I do from here?"

"Well, let us see… I think that for the first two hundred years or so, it should be fine to have you live here as a regular human. After that, we will bring you to reside in the divine realm. You will still be the custodian of this world, of course, and can freely visit it now and then."

"How exactly am I gonna go about managing the world?"

I was a bit concerned about looking after an entire planet when I had to rely on so many others just to keep my country together.

"I do not believe you will need to do much at all. You would only really need to interfere if the world barrels down a dangerous path or if it is threatened with imminent destruction."

"And what should I do in that case?"

"I imagine you would grant a sacred blade to someone you designate as messiah, or perhaps you could give some kind of divine guidance to the devout. You will not be able to directly interfere, as that would be a violation of the rules. Though, you could always circumvent this by assuming human form and descending to their world."

I was pretty glad to hear I wouldn't have too many responsibilities, but I really didn't want the world to deteriorate to the point where direct intervention became necessary.

"Well, we need not worry about that for now. This world is in your hands at this time, and that is a good thing. I mentioned earlier that I wished for this place to become something of a resort for the divine, do you recall? Keep this between us two, but a great many gods have expressed interest in the idea. There is quite the waiting list for deities requesting time off to enjoy themselves here."

"Is that gonna be okay? I don't know how well the world'll adapt to a bunch of gods chilling down here."

"Fret not, we will screen all the applicants carefully. They can only descend after converting into human form, anyway. Even if they run rampant, the world should remain safe. Ultimately, they only want to live an ordinary life for a while down here. Well... as ordinary as they can be. There is novelty in living out life as a regular human for a while. It is somewhat like those video games you had back on your original world."

That made sense to me. Video games were a great form of escapism. You could be a hero in an RPG, or lucky with the ladies in a dating sim, or even uncover mysteries as a detective in point-and-click games. The gods were keen to live a life that was unlike their everyday ones. It was a little funny to think about it like that.

I wondered if they were a bit jealous of Karen and the others.

"The god of love and the god of blades will stay to support and mentor you, as will the god of agriculture and the others. Is this all right?"

"I won't say no, but it kinda feels like you're giving me the favoritism you just told me you couldn't give..."

"Ohoho, I am sure nobody will mind, so long as we keep it implicit. The last time I had a direct benefactor was hundreds of billions of years ago, and I rather enjoy it. I would like to see you grow. Consider this an expression of familial love... Or the love of a grandfather for his grandson."

I was thankful that God Almighty cared about me so much, but I had a feeling all these gods on the ground were going to be a pain in my butt.

"Well, it will all come together in the end. Ah, one last thing… No world lasts forever. All come to an end with time. That applies to this world, and your former world as well. What is important, at the very end, is what kind of world it was. I hope that the fruits of your labor make other gods comment on what a splendid place it was when the end finally comes. And I hope that the god of destruction never has to visit this place on official business."

"Yeah. I don't want that to happen either…"

"I am sure you will do well, my boy. I'll be watching, and waiting, warmly."

Just like that, God Almighty vanished before my eyes. The sun had risen before I'd even noticed, illuminating the surrounding area.

I'm this world's custodian…

It honestly didn't feel real. Still, I had a couple hundred years to live as a regular human, so I wanted to start doing regular human things.

First thing's first…

"Hmm… I'm not sure about this one… What do you think, Lu?"

"Umm… I like frills, to be honest… I'd also love it if it had Regulus' national colors."

"Ooh. This is rather outrageous, it is. But perhaps I would be better suited to this one, I would…"

"This one looks good for moving in, Yae. I've seen this kind of style in Lestia before."

"Too much choice... Don't like this... I'll just choose one randomly..."

"Sakura, you can't choose something so important at random! You'll regret it later on."

"Please keep out of the way, Paula. You won't need a dress."

"Aw geez... This is so tough."

My fiancees were currently hard at work flipping through a big book of wedding dresses.

That was natural, given this was a once-in-a-lifetime opportunity for them. Personally, I thought they were making too big of a deal out of it, but I wasn't stupid enough to say that out loud.

"You just gotta go with what you feel! I chose mine right away!" Sue was sitting by me on the couch, shrugging as she spoke bluntly.

She had indeed chosen her dress right away and passed the photo on to Lapis, our chief maid. I kind of wanted to tell her to consider it a little more, but Sue was the kind of person who typically knew what she wanted at a glance.

"It's the wedding soon! I'll finally be able to call myself your wife. Isn't that amazing?" Sue laughed and gave me a tight hug from the side as she said that. She'd certainly changed the most compared to the first time I met her. She hadn't grown much in terms of size, but she was maturing at a fair rate.

In all honesty, there were still parts of me that viewed her as a kid, but then she'd come out with something that took me aback, and I realized just how much she'd grown.

In terms of my world's years, she was in her mid-teens. She was also around the same age that this world considered childhood to be over, so it was just a case of accepting the reality I was in. I was hardly an adult myself, after all.

"I feel a little bad about marrying Sue when she's this young... I get worried about how Duke Ortlinde's taking it."

"Don't worry, Touya! My parents are busy with little Edo, anyway. I love that little cutie too, he's such a good boy."

The Edo in question here was Edoward Ernes Ortlinde, Sue's little brother. He was the heir to Duke Ortlinde's household and my future brother-in-law. He wasn't even a year old yet.

Once I married Sue and the others, I'd gain a whole host of in-laws, but the only ones younger than me were Ed and Yumina's little brother Yamato. I kind of wondered how my relationship with them would be in the future.

Edo had a lot of hopes resting on him, and I hoped that he'd grow up to be a competent right-hand man to Yamato, the future king. It was kind of funny that Yamato and Edo ended up having Japanese-sounding names, but that was more a coincidence than anything else. Edo was just a nickname.

"When we get married, I can live here! I'll be with you dawn to dusk! Isn't that great?"

"It's great, yeah. I'll be happy to have you living here full-time, Sue."

"I've been doing a lot of preparation at home! I learned about sewing and cooking! All my tutors said nobles don't need to learn that stuff, but I want you to eat my cooking! And I want my children to have handmade clothes as well! I wanna do my best!"

Sue was the type to undertake a task and then see it through to the end. There wasn't much to read with her, since she was just straightforward and honest. The thought of her taking that kind of initiative for the sake of our future made me smile, and I hugged her back.

"No fair... Me too..." Sakura grumbled slightly as she walked toward me. It seemed like she'd chosen her dress as well.

"Did you pick out a dress?"

"Not gonna worry about it... Inside's more important than outside... Hug me... Hug me..." Sakura said as she held her arms out, giving a little pout in the process. I laughed a little before reaching out and embracing her as well.

There was definitely part of Sakura that enjoyed being pampered. She would definitely deny it if I brought it up, but I had a feeling daddy issues could've been at play there. She never knew her father during her childhood, so she probably had some repressed or unfulfilled feelings of wanting to be doted on by a fatherly figure.

To be honest, I wished she'd direct some of that need toward her actual dad, though. The overlord was so pathetic that it just made me cringe. I wondered if you could even call it daddy issues if the person with the issues didn't direct them toward her dad. Still, I knew at least that Sakura loved me as an equal. That was only part of her.

"Sakura's so spoiled."

"He's my husband... I can be a little spoiled... It's normal, especially when he's older..." Sakura matter-of-factly replied to Sue. That reminded me, every one of my wives except Leen was younger than me.

Yae and Hilde were a year younger. Elze and Linze were two years younger. Sakura was three years younger. Yumina and Lu were four years younger... And Sue was six years younger.

I knew that it wasn't exactly the same as how things were in my world, but I still had some reservations about being an eighteen-year-old about to marry a twelve-year-old.

Technically, Sue was sixteen in my calendar... but she sure didn't look like it. I couldn't tell if that was because people in this world aged slower or if it was because of my divinity influencing her.

Apparently, my divine benefactors would age up until a certain point and then stop growing, kind of similar to what happened with Leen and the other fairies. Sadly for Leen, her growth already stopped a while back, so she'd just stay the same regardless.

After a few years, it was entirely likely that Leen would look like the youngest of all my wives.

"When are we holding the ceremony...?"

"The world's still recovering, so probably not for half a year. We need to work hard on a lot of stuff right now, anyway," I gave a casual reply to Sakura's question.

We'd start preparing for the wedding while everything else was going on, but my current priority was dealing with Isengard. It wasn't really a functional country at this point. It was just a barren wasteland like Yulong. The only good thing about that bad situation was the presence of the puretree.

The spirits that had fled the country thanks to the divine venom were slowly coming back because of the puretree's allure. It would eventually become a landmass with a great number of spiritual inhabitants.

The main issue was deciding who that territory belonged to. Nothing had happened yet, but I didn't want a Yulong situation where people started laying claim to the remnants of the country. It was kind of good that the witch-king didn't produce any heirs, come to think of it.

All I could do was hope the three bordering nations, Lassei, Gardio, and Strain, would keep a close eye on the situation.

"Mmm... You're thinking about complicated stuff again. Forget about that and pay attention to us, Touya!"

"Sue's right... Pay attention..."

The two of them started chanting "pay attention" over and over after that. I didn't know whether to smile or feel freaked out.

It was definitely true that I'd been too busy for quality time in recent months, though. The issue with the wicked god had finally been squared away, so I did want to make it up to my wives... But I also had a lot of duties on the backburner.

"Well, I guess I can take the afternoon off."

I smiled and took out my smartphone, projecting its display into the air.

"We gonna watch a movie?"

"Yeah. Looks like the others are taking their sweet time, so let's watch something in the meantime."

"Okay... I wanna watch something funny... No horror movies..." Sakura made her needs known. I showed everyone a horror movie once and they freaked the hell out. It was pretty bad, honestly. Though it was a little bit funny seeing them scramble, given that they were born in a world with real zombies and wraiths out there.

"Hmm... Let's go for something simple."

The smartphone was a sacred treasure, and it actually translated any movie into the common tongue through divine means. But even if we had the language barrier cleared, that didn't mean the girls would be able to understand a movie that relied on too many foreign concepts.

Like, if I showed the girls a movie about the high-flying lives of the men on Wall Street, they wouldn't understand it. Though, I had a feeling maybe Doc Babylon would understand it more than I did.

I settled on a nice comedy. It was a simplistic story, but a classic one that was easy to pay attention to. It was the story of a piglet that learned how to herd sheep. If I recalled correctly, it was highly regarded and had a heartwarming ending.

"All right, it's starting."

"Hurray…"

I sat, sandwiched between Sue and Sakura, and decided to relax for the first time in a long while. It was nice to just take it easy for once.

As an aside, the girls did end up picking out their dresses. The movie was almost over by that point, so I restarted it to give them a chance to enjoy it as well. It was a lovely, happy scene.

Well, here we are at the end of *In Another World With My Smartphone* volume 19. I hope you liked it.

The showdown with the wicked god finally concluded in this volume. It took quite a while, huh?

There's a lot I want to say, honestly. I'm just not sure how to put it.

From the start, I had this idea in mind that the final fight needed to involve everyone who'd helped the heroes along the way.

I wanted to mix the smartphone into the message, conveying the idea that being connected to each other through them can make the world a better place. Thus, the title, *In Another World With My Smartphone*, would have come full circle by having Touya connect the other world with his smartphones.

I'm pretty happy that my original intentions came through in this part.

Hm? I know I said "final fight" just now, so you might be confused. I mentioned this in the last volume, but this isn't the end of the series. Thankfully, I can continue it.

After this, we'll see how the two worlds continue to adjust to their new merge, we'll see Touya's wedding, and the honeymoon. Stuff like that. I hope you stick with us through all that.

Now then...

This volume also has a special edition release in Japan. Hopefully people enjoy the Drama CD that it comes with.

The first drama CD we released was incredibly popular. We even had to issue a reprint. And thanks to that, we got to make a second one. I'm really glad it was so well-received.

It's already been two years since the anime ended, so it's nice to hear Touya and the others speaking again.

One thing that really excites me about the new CD is that the last three heroines are finally voiced! They only appeared in one wordless scene during the anime's run, so I'm very happy to hear them all together.

For this volume, I wanted to consider the story pacing, so I didn't really make any rewrites and I didn't add any original content. In all honesty, I haven't had a whole lot of free time, either. I've been working hard on my new series!

That's right, *In A Virtual World With My Bunny Scarf* volume 1 should be releasing in Japan at the same time as this volume.

I like to word my titles in a way that makes them identifiable at a glance, so I tend to use "In X with my Y" as the general style. My other book is a funny little story about a game world, as well as the players in the real world. If you ever get a chance to check it out, I hope you enjoy it.

Now then, it's time to give my thanks.

Eiji Usatsuka, your illustrations are wonderful as ever. Thank you for sticking with me on this long road, and thank you for your ongoing support.

I'd also like to give my special thanks to K, and everyone else involved at the Hobby Japan editorial department.

And, naturally, I'd like to thank you, my readers. Thank you to everyone who's followed my work since Shousetsuka ni Narou, and also all the newer light novel fans.

Fuyuhara Patora

In Another World With My Smartphone

Patora Fuyuhara
illustration・Eiji Usatsuka

20

VOLUME 20
ON SALE
FEBRUARY 2022!

By the Grace of the Gods

6

Roy
Illust. Ririnra

VOLUMES 1-6 ON SALE NOW!

Infinite Dendrogram
Art: Kami Imai
Original Story: Sakon Kaidou
Original Character Designs: Taiki
MANGA OMNIBUS 3
ON SALE NOW!
Omnibus
3

My Friend's Little Sister Has It IN for Me!

vol. 1

Author:
mikawaghost

Illustration:
tomari

**Volumes 1-2
On Sale Now!**

© tomari

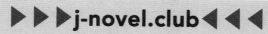

J-Novel Club Lineup

Ebook Releases Series List